MW01052723

TURNAROUND CEO

CEO

BECOMING THE CHANGE EXECUTIVE OFFICER IN CHARGE OF TURNING ANYTHING AROUND IN YOUR LIFE NOW!

Dr. J. Konrad Hölé

VIP
VISION IMPRINTS PUBLISHING
A Thomas Nelson Company
www.thomasnelson.com
Tulsa, Oklahoma

Published by Vision Imprints Publishing, Inc.
8801 S. Yale Ave, Suite 410
Tulsa, OK 74137
918-493-1718

Unless otherwise noted, all Scripture quotations are taken from the Scripture reference's taken from the Geneva Study Bible. Used by permission.

ISBN:0-849919-25-8
Library of Congress catalog card number: 2005933278

Printed in the United States of America

Contents

Special Thanks . . .

To Marianne Vugteveen, thank you for keeping your time spent in repairing this file from everything from computer freezes to the unpredictability that computers love to do; most of all keeping everything backed up.

To Lourdes Hudson—I have taught for years on the secrets of changing seasons in life, understanding times of transition, et cetera. . . . And one of the greatest truths I have ever discovered in this is the reality of how in every season of life that God schedules, He also schedules specific people to facilitate it. This is not as easy to follow as it sounds. Thank you enormously for being obedient to God to help facilitate the season of this book.

To Chris Ortiz, a very integral part of my circle; your ability to separate the truth from the familiar, or the person, is uncommon. You have provoked me to good works. Thank you for being everything you are regardless of what it costs you. If there is one thing I have learned in life, it is that none of us cannot network our way to significant change. People who can help cannot have an agenda. They must simply have answers. Thank you for having answers.

To my incredible children, Max and Sophia. Children are the leadership school from God. The only proof that we love a child is in how far we are willing to go to improve ourselves in order to develop them. So, you both definitely make Dad want to continually raise his game.

To God my Creator and heavenly Father and the ultimate CEO. While I spend hours every week teaching, counseling, consulting, and writing about the great mysteries and myths of leadership and human dysfunction, still I can only acknowledge after all is said and done, that while so much of personal turnaround is our choice and our vision, there is so much of it that does not work unless You make it work. There are the parts that we carry regardless of education, wealth, or influence that do not get lifted from us unless You lift them. Regardless of background or religion, You alone are worthy of all eminent power and glory and dominion for You being You alone. Thank you.

A Word from the Author

Why I wrote this book . . .

The great football coach Vince Lombardi stated that "Leaders are not born. They are made."

None of us can learn leadership. Boy, don't I feel stupid considering all of the years I have spent lecturing about it. *We can only learn to govern ourselves.* That is the core of personal leadership. As a matter of fact, that is the only type of leadership that exists on planet earth; *the leadership of ourselves.*

Personal leadership does not know place, or environment. You know how some people want to excel in the work place, but have zero capacity to lead at home or in parts of their personal lives?

You know where Hollywood stars can emanate better love relationships on the big screen, than they can in real life? You know where CEOs want to manage millions, but cannot even grasp how to manage their own self-esteem?

Personal leadership only knows the integrity system of YOU! Master it and anyplace YOU are, YOU will lead like a pro.

Inside of personal leadership everything comes down to a decision: *yours.*

But when all is said and done and the conference staff is cleaning up the mess from the mega seminar that you just paid big bucks to attend or when you finally put down the self-help or rags-to-riches bestseller you just purchased at the local bookstore, all things point to just one thing, what pain, rejection, failure, betrayal, miscalculations, oversights, and most of all character flaws are you going to grow past in order to lead by authority and not just title?

It's kind of like Al Pacino asking Keanu Reeves in the movie *The Devils Advocate*, "Can you summons your focus at will?" Can you summons an internal steel at will and overcome pain, rejection, failure, betrayal, miscalculations, oversights, and most of all your own character flaws?

Or are you just going to blame, then build a paradigm and a set of coping skills that justifies why it was okay to settle for less than what you were purposed to live?

You can only turn something around if you can turn around who you are in the midst of it.

You cannot turn around a company unless you can turn around YOU.

You cannot turn around a troubled marriage unless you can turn around YOU.

You cannot turn around years of destructive lifestyle or loss unless you can turn around YOU.

I am an ordained pastor. But this is not a religious decision. It is not even a cultural decision. It is a YOU decision.

People are only different because of their decisions, not their problems. Background does not separate us. Only game plan does.

Turnaround has no color; only submitted students. Turnaround has no favorites; only memorials of those who have paid the price to embrace it.

Turnaround does not care who did what to you. It only knows the person you are purposed to be and the depths in life you are called to reach.

My childhood abuse was not worse than somebody else's, so therefore my excuses cannot be bigger than everyone else's.

My gifts and skills are not enough to sustain me. They can only promote me. The foundation underneath my gifts is only what determines either my continued success or my eventual self-destruction.

I will never be so successful that I can fit in anywhere. Unscrupulous people have to resent me or I am just like them.

I believe you have as good of a chance as anyone at taking your game to the next level.

As much as I appreciate when someone uncommon brainstorms with me over how I can take my life to the next level, I equally appreciate you allowing me to spend the next several pages brainstorming with you.

Keep moving forward . . .

J.Konrad

Leadership is never just about the ability to lead others. It is about the ability to lead yourself first and let others follow.

1

YOU WILL HAVE TO PUSH YOURSELF BY YOURSELF.

Abusive leadership is when we assume that we can take others to the next level by teaching them to be the opposite of where we are not working to take ourselves to the next level first.

The racecar industry calls it drafting. It's when the lead car pulls all of the other cars around the racetrack.

This allows the other cars to save their gas, their engine pressure, and be protected from the turbulence that only comes by driving at the head of the pack.

People live their lives like this every day. They pull in behind everyone else driving at the head of the pack and they get drafted around the track of life by everyone else's intensity, dreams, identity, morality, commitment, passion, and purpose. Most of all they get drafted right into everyone else's victories without ever really achieving any of their own.

One reason is because it takes identity to be the lead car. So, less driven people will not battle with an energy problem as much as an identity one.

This is also a secret about driven people. *Driven people go after things because of how long they refuse to live life without them.*

It's kind of like one day when I met up with some friends and they asked me what I did on one of my recent days off. I said that I went shopping and ate at one of my favorite restaurants and then went to a sports bar to watch a baseball game for a while. Almost immediately someone in the group asked, "Who did you go with?" My answer was, "Just myself." My family was out of town.

Then the next response was, "You mean you did all that by yourself? I could never go to all of those places just by myself."

A large portion of society lives like that. Because of where they want to be, they live by who pulls them and who escorts them more than by where they will pull themselves.

This way they do not have to put their own necks on the line about anything significant, even at the times when something has broken down and must be restructured.

With no drive, all we do is end up placing unrealistic expectations on other people to please us as compensation for the lifestyle of fulfillment that we should be captivated to live ourselves.

The problem however is that when these people disappoint us, since we have nothing too captivating about our own dreams and goals to motivate us past our letdowns, we are then left to live life sitting around. Waiting of course for what other more ambitious, driven people will give us and fearful of what they won't; all the while mad at what we are too passive to give ourselves.

CEO FACT:

When other people drive us, we are forced to take on the identity of where they want to go. And nothing deteriorates us as badly as shrinking to live as the alter egos of other people's purposes .

People can encourage you, but you will have to push you. People can help you up, but you will have to pull yourself up.

This is one reason why people do not maintain their victories—*they never fought to achieve them.*

They arrived at whatever type of victory that they could manipulate using someone else's victories to facilitate for them. And the moment you explain your life through other people's progress, all you will really be explaining is your own helplessness.

The problem, however, with helplessness is how badly you set yourself up for disappointment and betrayal because of how badly you need whoever is drafting you to be the parts of your identity and backbone that they were never created to be.

One reason is because *people do not just link with us. They empower us.* The danger, however, comes when what we want to be empowered to become is everything that another person should never be permitted to give us. And since it is impossible for any person to empower both our sobriety and our self-deception at the same time, it is at these places that we will use right people for where we want to grow and wrong people for where we don't.

Then there is the other problem that gets mixed into all of this that comes from the type of people who agree to draft us; they are never healthy people . . . *they are control freaks.*

Meaning, the only reason they agree to draft us is because in drafting us they are able to live out their own hurts and hang-ups through our situations.

Stronger, healthier people on the other hand will never agree to drive you. They will provoke you and teach you to drive. Or they will leave you sitting on the shoulder of the road.

CEO FACT:

None of us qualify for what we want, until we are willing to go after it alone.

The only proof of desire is pursuit. The only proof of what you want in life is in what you will build every day of your life around obtaining.

It is always easiest to know where we live co-dependent on other people to drive us, because that is where we also live the angriest at where they can't.

So, we rate our own dreams and goals based on how much other people love us just for having some rather than on how we go after them on days when we're the only ones moving the train.

CEO FACT:

You will never be a good restarter unless you are a good self-starter.

The diet and exercise industries are both billion dollar entities simply because of how hard it is to get back on track with them even when you have gone away from them for just a few days.

Our human reaction is never to return to the scene of a failure. So, we will start something new rather than conquer something inconsistent.

Being a self-starter only requires that we do not need to have the right life before we can start moving towards a right destination. Being a restarter only requires our willingness to get over the disappointments from the things that did not go the way we thought they would that can only be used as hooks to derail us down the road if we don't. So in reality, none of us are ever stopped because of how big an obstacle is more than how big our personal resolve for what is on the other side of an obstacle is not.

CEO FACT:

Champions go to the top with or without the approval of others. Those who walk on water never ask those still sitting in the boat why they should.

Champions do not get driven. They drive.

It is when someone has to drive you that they can drive you to someplace you were not called to go.

It's not that champions do not ask for help, they just don't ask for approval. They do in fact depend on the strengths of others. They just don't wait for the strengths of others to validate every step before they take it. And where faith works is only for the things you are driven for and not the things you are always happy about. So, you will only wrestle with depression where you wrestle with the laziness to make strategic adjustments.

It is somewhere on the brink of your greatest increase that you will have to push yourself past your greatest disappointments. It's just that to tap the prosperity on the other side of any conflict, you will not be permitted to be better at being hurt than you are at making decisions to keep moving forward.

CEO FACT:

Deciding forward progress will only be as fast or slow as your willingness to discern your delays.

All of us encounter delays. But not all of us know what to use them for. No, this is not about being delayed in traffic so here are a few tips on utilizing the time. It's just that most people were taught that delays were a sign to become more stubborn than insightful.

So, while resolve is needed for not running from an obstacle, insight is what is needed for running over one.

That is what delays are. *They are signs, not stresses.*

Delays have a voice. They tell us what is missing or what is out of order. Delays are the proof of something that is not coming together.

Delays are not a sign that something is impossible but rather that something is missing.

Delays are not the proof of opposition. They are the proof of reposition. Opposition in anything cannot occur without telling you what is wrong.

Some days delays will tell you who or what you have no business pursuing. Other days you are in fact going after something right but using the wrong approach, the wrong plan, the wrong timing, the wrong people, or the wrong location.

Here will be some of your biggest delays.

1. **Unrealistic Relationships.** You cannot use wrong people to get to right places. People will not always stall you because they are bad, but rather because you are trying to carry them somewhere they are not supposed to go or you are depending on them to facilitate something that you believe they should, but they can't.
2. **Goals.** Goal delays will either expose an unnecessary goal or an unprepared one.
3. **Unrealistic plans.** Unachieved goals will only follow unrealistic plans. So, you will know when a plan is out of place by how draining or destructive it is to facilitate.

4. **Bad timing.** You will know right timing by favor and wrong timing by stress and lack.
5. **Faulty paradigms.** Every delay in your life will come down to a defect in your wisdom first.
6. **Bad boundaries.** You will fail once because of a boundary you did not have. You will fail twice because of a boundary you either would not enforce or restructure.
7. **Selfish decisions.** Selfish decisions protect pain and fear. Healthy decisions protect purpose.

Right decisions will flourish you. Selfish decisions will deplete you.

It is easy to recognize a selfish decision because of all the eventual lack, deterioration, and stress from a lack of progress that you will have to manage just to defend such a decision.

1.

Get ruthless about shrinking the amount of time that you have to be stuck, idle, or lost.

It's the long drawn out process that you turn your ditches into that becomes the greater problem than just the fact that you were even in a ditch.

Driven people do not treat a pothole like it is the Grand Canyon. They will not spend more time explaining a ditch than they do finding a tow truck.

Again . . . driven people go after things because of how long they refuse to live life without them. So, with no drive you are just a codependent person stuck with the unrealistic expectations you place on other people to please you as compensation for the type of lifestyle you should be captivated to reach for yourself.

➤ *You will have to bounce back quickly from anything disappointing or else your pain will shut the windows of opportunity that God gives you to move forward.* Talented people do not bounce back; driven people do.

Having to bounce back will protect your potential. Not your pride. Bouncing back determines what you learn; not how you look.

➤ *Make your mistakes your biggest classroom.*

People hate learning from their mistakes because they want to treat their weaknesses as personal rejection.

So while success is the result of what we've mastered, mistakes are the result of what is still mastering us. So while all adversity interrupts, it is not what beats us; passivity or indifference does.

2.

Every problem you will ever have in getting to the next level will only be in the areas where you do not want to be challenged.

Vision does not prevent apathy, conflict does.

Conflict in leadership is not about fighting enemies. It is about fighting narrow-mindedness; *your own.*

That is why we only can work through anything to the level that we allow ourselves to be challenged in. It is where we draw the line at personal challenge that we will change scenery before we will change a defect.

Which means where a leader does not want to be challenged he/she will only connect with other people as weak as them.

3.

Learn to consult the voice of opposition, more than just resent it.

Anyone can become stressed at delays. Not everyone can get insight as to the reasons why they exist.

Opposition will stop you from moving towards something wrong more than it will prevent you from moving towards something right. So, your only problem will be refusing to see the difference.

It is easier than not to tell what any season of change is trying to establish by looking at the type of warfare we are experiencing. *Warfare is always the clue of something that has been exposed for growth.*

So, wherever you are being tested the most is just the proof of where the person you are purposed to be is demanding more out of you than the person you are. So learn to step back just long enough to interrogate your opposition more than you just threaten it or hate it because it will not cooperate better.

➤ *Delays will never lie about what they reveal. So, don't attempt to turn what is cut and dry into what is gray, just because you're in fear.*

Gray is never what people see first. It is what people create when they fear the black and white that they do see. So, to see the reality of any situation or any obstacle, you will have to decide how much of your gray you are willing to restructure into what must be black and white.

Remember: *opposition can never occur without revealing what it is using.* So if you don't have any plans of conquering a giant in your life, you also will have no plans of interrogating what your giants could be telling you about how to conquer them.

4.

How comfortable are you with delays?

People can get comfortable with delays because of how much a delay can take the attention off of where they are not stepping up to take control of the leader they are not being inside of the delay.

Remember. Delays can be a relief because of how much they empathize with passivity.

They will also expose your resolve between talking versus doing. So it is easy for people to protect delays when they are really protecting fear. Fear is what we cope with when our lives are built around waiting for what we hope a delay will resolve for us on its own. And anger is what we cope with when our lives are dictated to by the waiting.

Where is your behavior or personal integrity off course with where you need to be in this area?

How would the person you want to be handle this area differently?

Leadership is never just about the ability to be strong; it is also about the ability to not be weak at the wrong times.

2

GOD DOES NOT MAKE LEADERS. HE PLACES MEN AND WOMEN IN LEADERSHIP SITUATIONS AND THEY EITHER STEP UP OR BACK DOWN.

This would explain why people only self-destruct because they fear success and they resent where success is demanding more from them than they thought they should have to pay.

Finishing your dreams and goals is never just about protecting your strengths. It is about not minimizing which one of your weaknesses that could sabotage your strengths and then protecting yourself from your own self-deception.

And for every leader there are three distinct dangers greater than any other.

1. When you lack the ability to recognize deterioration.

2. When you assume that the deterioration is not what it really is or that you have more time than you actually have before you need to fix it.

3. When you blame things that are lacking in your leadership as though they are really things lacking in your resources or circumstances.

This is why leadership is never what position makes us. As a matter a fact, it is not even what education makes us. It is what conflict makes us the moment we choose to lead more than care-take.

This also describes leadership self-destruction as being the places where we back down at the moment it is time to stand up. So, just find the places where you turn opportunities to conquer new ground into an opportunity to allow chaos or self-destruction to become your smokescreen for embracing neutrality, and you will find the places where you shut down when it is time to lead.

CEO FACT:

Leadership is never what good times make you. It is what you refuse to allow passivity to make you during anxious times.

Winners want the ball when the game is on the line.

Losers only want the ball when their ego is on the line.

Regardless of government presidents or soccer moms, when passive leadership is the route of choice, it will be impossible not to manipulate other people to do your dirty work for you.

This is called dictatorship. *Dictatorship is not the presence of strength. It is the presence of insecurity. Dictatorship is not the demonstration of power. It is the offering of power in exchange for the protection of position.*

Government leaders to corporate leaders do this as easily as parents and husbands and wives. It is the embracing of weakness in tough times that hooks you as an addict to the intensity of others in order to be pushed into decisions that you wished you could make on your own, but are too afraid to.

The reason fear is involved is not always because these are right decisions. Often times we fear getting caught for making selfish decisions because we fear not being perceived as a better person than selfish.

Therefore, it becomes easy to manipulate the weaknesses in certain people as our own empowerment in making weak decisions.

However, the only thing worse than your refusal to deal with a giant on your own strength, will be assuming that you can discard personal integrity to enable the strengths of others to remove the giant for you. This is called empowerment.

And as mentioned from Chapter 1, empowerment is different than just normal influence. We cannot say that all empowerment is bad. But when it is used for bad it is always in the places where our codependence is compensating for a toxic lack of personal leadership.

That is what defines the average empowerment relationship: when we trade our problems with identity and a lack of character for someone else's deficient problems with identity and lack of character, but who are much more driven and sophisticated in the calculation of presenting their dysfunction as normal and right.

These are people who have had more experience at making issues of fear and control look more self-serving and less toxic than they really are. Really these people are just more hardened than us.

In human connections we cannot be lead by our weaknesses and expect to connect with any other kind of people other than those who will exploit us for having weaknesses.

This explains the core of codependence. Codependence is never the lack of self-leadership; it is the fear of self-leadership.

It is in our codependent areas that we are so ripe to become converts of those more driven but yet just as deficient people as ourselves. This is because of how much they portray their poison as charming, at times glamorous, and most always very liberating and not to mention okay.

This is also how you know negative empowerment from right influence. *Negative empowerment always centers around and protects self-centeredness. Whereas positive influence always defends the truth even when the truth does not line up with which parts of your agenda are built around being self-centered.*

And let's point out one issue. Being self-centered does not mean we are bad people. Self-centeredness is the protection of pain and fear. However, this is also how we connect with negative empowerment; we determine the level of selfishness we want to get away with based on our hurts, fears, and greed. Then we determine whose own toxic pain and hang-up induced paradigms are big enough to justify our course of action and hide, in part, our decisions inside of their advice.

These people help coach us to take steps for self-gratifying reasons when we are afraid to grow past manipulation, deception, or revenge to take any other steps other than self-protective ones.

The danger however is that most of these types of people never officially tell us to jump off the cliff. They just help us get to the edge while only giving us the impression that we should jump.

Then when we jump, while on the way down, we discover that not only did we jump alone, but these people refuse to be held accountable for their advice. And guess what? They are not at the bottom to catch us either.

Remember this: *Sound wisdom will promote issues of forgiveness, reconciliation, and faith. It will move you forward. It will not justify selfishness all in the name of protecting personal pain.*

CEO FACT:

You will only turn weak where you don't mind functioning by selective sight.

The greatest anger you will live bound by will be the anger from the problems you are not solving because they are the problems you are afraid to look at.

Which is why the beginning of any solution to a problem always begins with solving our fear of the problem first. Only because people see what they want to see. So we only solve any problem to the degree that we want to see it and to the degree that we want to see ourselves within the problem.

Judging yourself does not require intelligence. It requires humility. So as a leader you cannot complain over being hurt if it was your own stubborn approach to disorder that set you up for the pain.

Which is also why personal deterioration is not about the inability to deal with a problem. It is about the refusal to see the reality of one.

So, selective sight becomes the protection of fear by using enough of your own logic to do it. The danger, however, is when your logic protects your passivity so much that it passes off what is destructive as normal or reasonable.

You see, most people don't live limited by problems they can't see, but rather limited by problems they refuse to see. So, it is not hard to find where anger resides in us the most, because anger always surrounds the resentment we have towards the things we wished we could refuse to tolerate but fear has convinced us would be too costly not to.

That is all that anger is . . . *the residue from believing we are trapped to coexist with fear.*

Fear does not promote sight. It distorts it. Distorted sight helps you feel safe, not alert.

Distorted sight helps you maintain self-deception, not self-sobriety, and does so through the fear that intimidates you with what the cost would be to solve a problem instead of just manage one.

CEO FACT:

People do not manage anger; they manage helplessness.

We manage helplessness by managing the traps that fear tells us we are not good enough to stop managing.

The term *"anger management"*? Pretty humorous. You cannot manage anger. You can only manage changes. There is no anger in change. Anger is only in what we are still facilitating about everything that is still not different. However the force of anger in any of us can strike at will. You cannot manage that. But what you can manage is your commitment to personal growth which in turn changes your angry approach towards anything painful.

That is what helplessness is. It is not the position of being stuck. Instead it is the lies we believe about the rut mixed with the lies we believe about where our outlook of ourselves is no better than the rut.

"But don't you have to acknowledge powerlessness to something before you can get help?" Not exactly.

I am not powerless to anything except where my own lack of healthy esteem and my wounded perspective tells me that I have to co-exist with the mediocrity I self-medicate. And since I only can medicate the abusive lies I believe, I am only powerless to self-deception . . . not an addiction.

Helplessness is never about the abuse we experience. *It is about the abuse we accept.*

Meaning it is about accepting a perspective that you must not be any better than the negative you repeatedly encounter.

However, where we do not enforce a rock solid code of personal leadership certain wounds, mistakes, addictions, et cetera, that really aren't as impossible to overcome as we think, are given size that they do not deserve simply because our own lack of self-decency gives it to them.

So as we will deal with later in this book, most people only get addicted to what they use in managing passivity. With self-destruction it is the same thing.

Self-destruction is not the fear of failure; *it's the fear of winning.* Which is why people who self-destruct do not self-destruct because of pain they cannot leave, but rather success they will not embrace.

CEO FACT:

Where you are not managing vision, you will be managing drama.

The only proof of having a vision for your life is what you will spend your time on. Visionaries spend their time going towards their vision. Whereas people with little to no vision just spend their time compensating for not having one.

Welcome to drama—*the chaos that we will permit so we can expend our creative energy on issues other than the plans to succeed that we are not pursuing.*

It's like this. You will never move forward with your life by being your own best soap opera. And you only create drama where you are not creating plans to succeed.

Drama is a self-protective mechanism that we use not because we love pain, but because we love what we can hide behind pain. But the only danger in loving the drama of pain is that we will create pain in order to cope with pain just to keep the game going.

Drama is a diversion. It is what we allow a problem to be because of everything that our vision for purpose is not. In other words, drama occurs not because we are experiencing a problem, but rather because we have become in love with our ability to inflate situations and permitted behavior as a means of placing something negative as a cover up for what is not being resolved.

And you will know when you love drama because you keep talking about problems you won't solve. Action never surrounds enormous discussion. Action is resolve. Whereas anger is just the reflection of a lack of action.

So, other people's problems are used to veil our own. Little things become big things. Immaturity that should have been dealt with a while ago is fueled instead to stay burning. All this for one reason—*to glorify the size of what neutralizes us, so we can maintain the excuses for why we are still no further down the road than we are.*

All drama is draining because it is not wisdom. It is emotion. So, there is no learning value, only experiential and reminiscing value. Experiencing anything does not necessarily change us. Reminiscing about pain or regrets only fuels our anger, not our understanding.

So it is not the emotion value that is wrong since we are created one third emotional. But drama is a game.

A game for people who need something to do when building a healthier and more successful them is not their game. So it is not surprising when we function with little to no inspiration to conquer new dimensions of personal growth because of how enchanted we have become with the game of avoiding growth.

CEO FACT:

Champions preach what they have lived. Losers only preach what they have heard.

Knowledge is what you get from another person's victories. Wisdom is what you get from your own.

And the only difference between wisdom and opinion is application.

1.

You will never make a leadership decision and a sentimental decision all in the same decision.

Progress in anything is a result of making leadership decisions regardless of whether or not they are popular ones.

Leadership decisions only know direction, not familiarity, circumstances or setbacks.

Leadership does not know nostalgia. It only knows leadership. This is because truth does not know bloodlines or heritage. It only knows truth.

➤ *Your decisions have to have a destiny attached to them.* Any leadership decision can only be made because of a destination you need to be at and not because of all of the nostalgia that surrounds where you are.

All sentimental decisions do is leave us wanting to take a stand for too many conflicting things so we can accommodate too many conflicting sides.

It is somewhere on the brink of your greatest changes you will have to make decisions because of what is right and not because of what is familiar.

For example, you cannot work a dead-end job because you have been working there for twenty years.

You cannot have abusive or incompetent people close to you just because you have known them since childhood or they are related. And, you cannot protect something that is incompetent just because at one point it was good.

That is what sentimentalism does. *It keeps us obligated to what cannot facilitate our future just because of the way things used to facilitate our past.*

Want to feel warm and fuzzy, then buy a dog. Want to keep your dreams and goals moving forward even on your darkest days, then you will have to know your end result from your warm and fuzzy.

2.

Stay out of the "if you could do it all over again, what would you do differently" trap.

Regret only fuels anger. We don't learn anything new in regrets. We only keep learning more about everything we still hate.

This is where a lot of our self-destructive rage comes from. The places where we feel like we are trapped to live with what we wished we would have done differently.

The one greatest reality is that THERE ARE NO REGRETS IN LIFE! There is only what we keep doing the same way and for the same reasons or what we have adjusted and are now doing differently.

Either way . . . *where a person lives with regrets is where they are really living with the pain of what is still the same.*

"But I regret I did not change things sooner." Well you didn't, so if you have now, then be happy. One reason for this is because faith does not connect you to yesterday; it only connects you to the future. So, regrets only fuel the depression from the anger over the past you cannot change.

This is where people either make changes or they make excuses, but never both. And when you make necessary changes then where you could have made those changes sooner becomes very irrelevant.

When you attempt to derive wisdom for yesterday, as many do when they want to justify their right to have regrets, what you are really doing is going somewhere not even God can go: *your past.*

It's like this: You cannot discuss the wisdom of what was broken, only what is fixed. So you will know true wisdom because it always moves forward from today, not yesterday. Yesterday should only fuel remorse.

Where is your behavior or personal integrity off course with where you need to be in this area?

How would the person you want to be handle this area differently?

REALITY CHECK

Leadership is not about changing scenery. It is about changing standards.

3

YOUR PROGRESS WILL NEVER BE THE RESULT OF WHAT YOU ARE WILLING TO ADD BEFORE IT IS THE RESULT OF WHAT YOU ARE WILLING TO REMOVE FIRST.

Nothing right in your life will produce the prosperity that it could until anything that could sabotage it is first removed.

Adding gym equipment does not help you if you will not remove junk food. Adding more money does not help you if you will not remove frivolous spending. You get the picture. *Life is an issue of subtraction before it is ever an issue of addition.* This is because pruning is only proactive, or else it is not pruning; it is hiding. So the only thing worse than your refusal to remove something unproductive is hoping it will leave on its own.

One reason is because you cannot get to the vision of a better you until you get a vision for changing what is contributing to the bad you. Anything you do not have the vision to change will become stuck in the delusion that assumes you can succeed long term in spite of it.

However some days before we can step into something, we will have to step out of something else. Meaning, a new season is not when you carry the old you into it.

Which is why on the brink of moving to a new level of growth, your limitations will use fear to negotiate with your passivity as a way to keep you where you are.

It's like this: *Pruning determines growth. Planning doesn't. Planning just reveals good intentions. Anything unproductive that we will not prune we will only allow to multiply in its dysfunctional state.*

So, nothing disorderly or destructive about us ever just goes away because we became better at avoiding it. It comes back later and dares us in a more turbulent and costly way to deal with it.

So, whether a destructive habit or a costly addiction, a distractive relationship or a faulty character defect, *failure is never the act of something bad we do more than the result of something bad we tolerate, and you will only tolerate anything destructive until failure strips you of an argument.*

CEO FACT:

Personal warfare will only last as long as it takes for what entered through weakness to now exit through strength.

An age-old question always surrounds the duration of certain conflicts. *"How much longer do I have to deal with this?"* Simple—*nothing bad ever leaves our lives until it leaves through something good.*

Which means you cannot use the uncharactered parts of you to defend the undeveloped parts of you and then be shocked when you are doing the same wrong things over again.

So, this becomes the myth about personal battles and adversities when we just assume that our battles only last as long as it takes us to outlast them. *Not accurate.*

Even traumatic experiences never leave us until they can leave through changes and improvements that are good.

This is why certain unhealthy behavior patterns can repeat themselves for years despite which parts of them we are innocent victims to. *We don't just move on because of what we survive. We change something about ourselves and then we move on.*

In other words, we only leave the conflicts that we have matured our way out of. There is no survival in change. Survival is what we live when we are not changing.

Which would explain why some of us are only provoked to grow by two means—*where we are driven to make change and where our personal weaknesses land us in situations that leave us no other choice but to change.*

So, our battles either end when the parts of us that are creating them or facilitating them end. Or, they just keep reinventing themselves in new places and new seasons of our lives.

This is where most conflict enters—*someplace weak.* No, having weaknesses does not mean that we have no strengths. But a weakness is the only place where we will justify compromise. Because it is also the place where we are too dependent on what we feel and not dependent enough on what we should believe.

Meaning, we are ruled more by what the conflict hurt in us, more than what the conflict exposed in us.

It is not even that feelings are wrong except that they never provoke us to reality, only what we wish reality is.

CEO FACT:

Your enemies will only be as effective against you as what you refuse to improve about yourself.

People fail in life because of how much they attempt to use their flesh to defend themselves against the destructive things that their flesh has no ability to say no to. So it is only the strategy of our perversions to keep us in a place where a weakness is forced to defend us. It can't. That's why it is a weakness.

This is also why a weakness is always the target of conflict because a weakness is the place of blindness. Any of us only fail because of our own blind spots, not someone else's. So weaknesses are where we control from a position of protecting pain in some form. With a weakness we will do more to protect safety than expose error.

So, blind spots are developed. Blind spots are as much the protection of fear as they are the absence of understanding. Inside of our blind spots are the parts of us void of enough truth to expose error.

So, while other people can help our fall, it will always be our present weakness in something that decided it.

Then vanity is brought into the mix.

Why? Because of what vanity is. Vanity is the delusion that what is perverted about us is really better than the obvious problems that we are experiencing as a result of it. Vanity is when we keep shooting ourselves but insist that the gun did not produce the wound.

CEO FACT:

Failure is a journey more than a destination. How you end up there is only the result of what you refused to deal with along the way.

You will never start at failure. You will end up there.

Failure is not an act. It is an end result. Failure is not the place where a leader will self-destruct. It is the culmination of what a leader was tolerating long before it brought them to the place of destruction.

One reason is because *leaders do not fail because of what they lack. They fail because of what they refused to restructure.*

So the reality is this: *before our defects can cause failure, they will cause misery and lack.* Meaning, we will allow something to produce misery and lack before we allow it to produce failure. Failure just becomes what forces us to get sober about where we're managing too much misery and lack.

CEO FACT:

Whatever you will not force the exit of, you will become.

Fear, anger, hate, unforgiveness, past abuse, strife, mediocrity, a compromised standard, a lie, indifferent employees, divisive behavior . . . whatever you cannot get rid of, you will become.

So, in my personal Sunday occupation of pastoring, often times formerly abused parishioners from previous churches will ask me, "How could a leader be so abusive to innocent people?" My answer is always simple—someone abused them.

We don't change what we hate. We become what we hate. So, the average person assumes that because they resent the way their parents raised them, they will just automatically raise their children differently. No so.

We only change things when we change our character to be different people.

You cannot change something that you hate because you resented it being done to you. You can only change something you hate because you build the character necessary to not perpetuate it. So, it becomes insanity to assume that you can control the worst experiences of you and not create your own worst conflicts.

That is what all change is. *It is not the presence of strength, but rather the intolerance of weakness.*

So, a bad experience, a bad teacher, a bad memory, or whatever continues to be carried by you just becomes what you are and what you will do to other people.

It is at this crossroad that we decide our fate.

To turn one way will determine what we repeat.

To turn another, will determine what we overcome.

So uncommon leadership is not about having less things to change. It is instead about taking less time to change them. So, some leaders will change things on a dime, whereas other leaders need an acre just to think about it.

Either way, your leadership is only as effective as how fast or slow you are willing to deal with what is unproductive, off course, or destructive.

CEO FACT:

Anything unhealthy that you cannot walk away from you will have to use the deception of denial to compensate for.

The entrance of dysfunction will not destroy you. Your unwillingness to deal with it will. So, you cannot use what is inappropriate and remove what is inappropriate all at the same time.

The fruit of learning can only be seen by application, not good intention. Which means all change comes down to one thing: *the refusal to settle.*

So, you can only determine success and failure by the types of unhealthy things you are willing to walk away from. Meaning what you will not remove will ultimately imprison you by the deception that circumstances and people have destroyed about you, what in reality only your own lack of character could.

People who stay victims, victimize. So, nothing unproductive changes until you stop participating with it. It's just that when God gives you the opportunity to change, He will also give you the opportunity to walk away from who, and what, was around you making your dysfunction appear normal.

And since the associations we permit will yield the results we will have to live with, what unprincipled people and unhealthy coping skills help you destroy they will never help you rebuild.

1.

Change what you are managing.

I will deal more on the topic of changing our lives by changing what we manage towards the end of this book. I cannot help but refer to this principle repetitively only because of how much this is the one most dramatic truth that I attribute to my most dramatic personal growth.

However, for now, *our lives can only repeat what we are built to go through good or bad.* Meaning where we have been negatively built to handle the chaos from self-destruction and mediocrity, then we can only keep anticipating the same results to happen in everything we get involved in.

So, in restructuring our lives around anticipating something better means we may have to make changes some days in the dark because of the lack of good reference points we have to draw from with the healthier way things are supposed to be.

So how do we stop managing?

➤ *Stop managing crutches.* Celebrities *(or those who wished they were)* bring huge entourages with them everywhere they go. People will dominate conversation or overuse humor to compensate for inferiority. Executives will do drugs to deal with pressure.

Crutches are the things we put in place for the purpose of upholding something that is broken. This works great for the busted ski accident ankle. But crutches are not boundaries. They are not outlets. They are the emotional vices built to manage inadequacy because of what is still deformed in us.

➤ *Manage your own changes only.*

When we manage other people's problems, we make their problems our own. Then we are forced to control their problems to not be a problem for us. That only makes us angry every time we feel guilty for why they still have a problem.

➤ *Stop managing traps.* All traps live and die by their ability to use the old you as fuel. Don't let them.

We don't keep stepping in traps because we don't know the traps. We step in the traps because we don't know who we are in the traps. So, when you manage a trap you are really managing the ignorance about yourself.

➤ *Make changes quick.* Yes, get unbiased council when needed, but stop *"doinking around" (my alternative word to the real word I wished I could use)* with enforcing change. The longer you dangle before submitting yourself to a necessary change, the more prone you will become to repeating an unnecessary setback.

Where is your behavior or personal integrity off course with where you need to be in this area?

How would the person you want to be handle this area differently?

Leadership is never learned in a classroom. It is learned on the battlefield by taking on what the average are trying to avoid.

4

YOU WILL NEVER CONQUER GIANTS BIGGER THAN THE PERSON YOU ARE WILLING TO BECOME.

We don't find giants on the level we are on. They are only on the levels that we are either pushing to get to or at least should be. Giants are never alongside of us. They are in front of us.

This is because *none of us conquer giants because of the person we are, but because of the person we are willing to become.* So when the same size giants can keep derailing us it is only because we are still the same size people.

Which is one reason why progress in anything is never about living without giants. Rather, it is about changing the size of the giants that can keep derailing us.

In other words, most people do not change the size of their battles. They just get sick of fighting. And we only get sick of fighting when all we are doing is fighting the same things on the same level. In other words, it's the same size giants that are only fought by using the same size blind spots. So, something has to change in you before something can be diminished about the kinds of enemies that can keep derailing you.

You will know when you are dealing with the same size giants because they keep digging the same size holes that you keep falling into and you keep being the same person using the same ineffective tools to dig your way out. In other words, what you keep handling the same way, you keep repeating the same way.

CEO FACT:

You will never kill a giant that you are glorifying the size of.

Being overwhelmed by a giant is never the problem. Being a worshipper of a giant is.

Success in anything is never because your obstacles become smaller but because the time that you spent resenting them, blaming them, complaining about them, or being overwhelmed about them becomes shorter.

So, while you may fall into a rut because of what an obstacle is, you will only stay in a rut because of what you have allowed an obstacle to become.

Worshipping a giant is the indicator you have accepted the giant. So, people only become worshippers of their giants for two primary reasons.

1. To mask their real fear of confronting them and their real anger from demanding more out of life then they are making healthy changes to get.

2. When their character to deal with the obstacle for what it is, is too weak not to call it anything else but impossible.

It's like this: none of us ever conquer a problem where we are always describing it as being just beyond our reach to really do anything serious about.

This is when the severity of the problem actually has turned into our excuse to leave it alone more than our wake up call to do anything about it. Part of learning to kill bigger giants will be your refusal to keep babysitting everything that is incapable of producing bigger victories.

So, you cannot increase a Fortune 500 company into a Fortune 100 company without first being able to recognize sooner than later who and what in the company is incapable of producing your increase.

You cannot take a losing team and produce a winning team until you can define who is currently on the team that cannot produce a championship.

Or you can look at it like this: *any hump you still cannot move past is only an indicator of something you are still using a dysfunctional approach to negotiate with.* Just look at any scenarios that you keep finding yourself back in again. *Repetitive chaos never lies.* It is always the fruit of what we have not changed yet.

This usually means that there is something we are defending rather than correcting when it comes to returning to these situations.

CEO FACT:

What you refuse to outgrow, you will be forced to purposely go backwards just to fit in with.

Most of us do not have a hard time deciding when to leave a bad situation. We only have a tough time deciding when to leave a dysfunctional us. In other words, you will never have to decide when to move on from anything or anyone; *your growth as a person will decide this. One reason is because growth immediately provokes space between us and whatever is not growing.* This is where you decide, *do I keep growing? Or do I slam on the brakes and fit back in with what I fear may not be growing with me?*

Either way, you cannot leave a negative situation until you can leave a weakness in you.

You cannot leave defective relationships until you leave a defect in you. You cannot leave a dead-end job until you leave a dead-end personal vision.

What you manage you will make space for and time to occupy. So, nothing changes with what you don't want until something changes with the parts of you that are managing everything wrong about it.

So, welcome to the secret of knowing when it is time to go to the next level. You become too cramped on the level you are at. No, not impatient . . . cramped.

Impatient just means you want to be further down the road than where you are. Cramped means you have grown too much to keep accommodating being where you are.

You will know when you are outgrowing the level you are on by how cramped it becomes to be there.

However, it is in this place of being cramped that you will either be confronted to take the steps necessary to finish the process of graduating to a greater level or you will purposely shrink just so that you can go back to being the size of person that you were when you entered your present level and thought that it was so spacious.

Either way, *our decisions always reveal what we are either outgrowing or fitting in with.*

So, if your behavior becomes more dysfunctional or your outlook becomes more selfish as the result of where you are trying to move on from, then either where you are moving to or the reasons you are moving there is not the answer you need it to be.

In other words, if you leave a marriage and become angrier or more self-absorbed, or if you move to a new state or a new job and become less productive, you just don't escape to a new level. You either outgrow who you have been and graduate to a new level or else you don't go there.

CEO FACT:

Your enemy will always fear your ability to learn from anything that was meant to destroy you.

Abuse was meant to destroy you.
Betrayal was meant to destroy you.
Abandonment was meant to destroy you.
A bad decision was meant to destroy you.
A bad divorce was meant to destroy you.
A bad accident was meant to destroy you.

A bad decision . . . the list goes on. *Battles are never won based on how you manage your enemy, but rather how you manage you.*

One reason is because any giant on any level can only be a giant as long as a weakness in you is participating.

The reality is that mediocre leaders are never worse off because they have been hurt more, but rather because they have recovered less.

So, in actuality, your defeat in anything will rarely be the result of a superior enemy more than your own superior stubbornness that is preventing you from being anything greater than the person you have always been in the same destructive battles.

1.

Ask yourself, "Am I still fighting the same old battles that I should have learned from years ago or am I fighting new battles that are facilitating the person I am called to be now?"

You will never be conflict free. But the same battles are only fought on the same level. So, if you want to change levels then you will have to change the size of the giants that you are willing to conquer.

We only fight the same conflicts because of what we have never changed about our perspective and approach from previous conflicts.

➤ *Take your approach out of the box and your victory will follow right behind.* Your behavior always says what you believe about something.

Defective responses to something only come from a defective awareness of it. So, your response to anything can only be as healthy as your perspective of it is.

Remember: *Any giant distracting you is safe as long as your own narrow perspective of the battle allows them to be.*

2.

Change what you see about your giants.

The average person only wants to see their giants differently after the injustices from being in a fight have been resolved. That's not how it works.

Conflict is the link to change. Conflict is never the proof you have an enemy. Rather, it is the proof you have a destiny. So, when your giants look the same size to you, then all you'll do is stay in the same battles.

It's like this: By the time King David became embroiled in dealing with a jealous king trying to kill him for no good reason, he had already lost any intimidation of seeing his first adversaries, a lion and a bear, the same way.

David transcended the size of the giants he could conquer because he first transcended how he chose to view yesterday's giants.

3.

Shrink the number of giants that stop you.

Giants only exploit what is sick in us . . . not what is healthy. So, no giant will ever do to you what you love yourself too much not to do to yourself.

What is sad is how many people engage themselves in the battle to improve, change direction, and make the radical decisions necessary, but do not even last in the conflict two seconds before getting floored and bewildered. It's not because of how big their giants are, but rather because of how many of them there are.

➤ *You cannot achieve million dollar dreams while giving a million different enemies the access to derail you.*

The more giants you make room for the bigger the battlefield you will have to provide for them to exist on until your focus, dreams, outlook, esteem, prosperity, et cetera, eventually die prematurely from exhaustion, depression, and bitterness.

The longer the list, the longer the detours.

➤ *Stop policing the people, distractions, hurts, thoughts, and the fights that are not on the level that you want to be on.*

Choose your fights for the level you want to be on, not the level you don't.

Where is your behavior or personal integrity off course with where you need to be in this area?

____

____

____

____

____

____

____

How would the person you want to be handle this area differently?

____

____

____

____

____

____

____

Leadership is defined as much by the people you avoid as it is the ones you embrace.

5

THE RELATIONSHIPS YOU PERMIT WILL DETERMINE THE STANDARD YOU DISPLAY.

Jesus used this principle to determine His relationships when He walked the earth. *Who can I be seen with? Who can't I?*

Jesus would be seen with the biggest sinners of His day, but whose hearts were ripe for change. But He would avoid the most religious elite of His day who professed no sin, but whose hearts were evil with pride.

Who we don't mind being seen with determines our values or lack of them.

No, this is not an issue of arrogance but rather a reality that whoever you are seen with allows everyone else to assume that you must believe the same way. So, the moment you declare your link with someone, you declare your approval of what they stand for.

None of us are ever bigger than the associations we keep. So with every relationship that we embrace there will be other associations in their life just like them.

With your blind spots, mutual blind spots provide mutual hiding. With your integrity, mutual integrity provides mutual increase. Just show me the character or lack of it with the people closest to you and I can show you the victories or defeats that you will repeat.

CEO FACT:

Prosperity or destruction are simply the result of who enters your life. Your only problem will be the inability to discern who has been sent for what.

Ethical people will only run with other ethical people because "iron sharpens iron" (Proverbs 27:17).

But unethical people will only run with other unethical people because there is no threat of truth to expose error. It's the person you choose to be that will determine the support system that you build around you to enable you to be it.

No, your bar does not need to be so high that only God Himself could like you, but people who love mediocrity need not love you.

I learned this lesson while speaking in North Carolina some years ago. At the end of my engagement there, I was to receive my honorarium.

When standing in the host's office he proceeded to inform me that he had changed the financial arrangements without first informing me, just because that is what he needed to do. If this was an issue of a lack of money, then I would have gladly obliged. But after seeing his two hundred dollar neckties and his eight hundred dollar alligator shoes, not to mention the Lexus he drove all of them around in, money was not the issue. Greed and deception were.

This of course became too obvious, the more irate he became the more I questioned his motives and reasons.

Nevertheless, I left with my newly reduced honorarium, only to later be scheduled to speak for a buddy of his in another state. I did not even make it there. Instead, this friend canceled my scheduled speaking engagement within days of my arrival there with no explanation and with no returned phone calls. Not to mention without any reimbursement for my already purchased airline ticket and the now too late to replace hole in my schedule.

After calming down I realized, *"Why am I surprised? Both of these two individuals are close friends. Why wouldn't they share the same lack of ethics?"*

Then what dawned on me further was the cold reality that this was why they were friends; *they protected the same deceitful conduct in each other.*

When we take on any relationship, we take their values too. So anyone we connect with can only teach us how to be just like them either good or bad.

And we never just connect to who other people are; we connect to who we are either good or bad in other people.

This is the other part of the connection fact: *Relationships never just connect through chemistry. Motive is involved also.* So when it comes to our connections to unprincipled or unscrupulous people, *we will only determine what connects us to such individuals when we acknowledge what we need them for.*

It's like this: part of removing unprincipled people is first removing in yourself why they like you.

Weak leaders use other weak leaders to run faulty companies. This is because we never practice a different standard with others than the one that we permit those closest to us to practice with us.

One reason is because *your relationships reflect you, not the other person.* So, you permit other people to store their disorder with you so that you can store your disorder with them.

CEO FACT:

The most dangerous people you will ever have in your life will be those comfortable with inaccuracy.

Exaggerators and divisive people are always one in the same person. Just like those who avoid confrontation and those who avoid truth are always one in the same person also.

People who are lovers of truth are not lovers of hearsay.

People who believe lies tell lies. Should I keep going?

It's like this: People who use exaggeration use lying also. Exaggerators are never into truth, only perception. So, people who cannot paint an accurate picture *for* you are never going to paint an accurate picture *of* you either.

Accuracy never requires damage control. Which is why accuracy is only feared by those who have mastered deception. This is also why one way to identify a deceiver is they never ask for truth more than agreement. One reason is because vague people never defend a side more than they defend their own fear.

This is also why accusation only blooms amongst the impressionable. Impressionable people are dangerous because they only require personality and presentation to influence them, not fact.

And the reality is that you will only be betrayed by those who can be sold on the unproven or enchanted by the unfortunate.

1.

Do not use nostalgia as loyalty to what may be unhealthy or expired.

Ah yes. The old *"but we go way back"* story. How way back people go with you only matters if you can go way forward with them.

In the process of raising your own game up a notch or two, it becomes as much of an issue of who you will fight to distance yourself from, as it is does who you will fight to work through conflicts with.

Anyone not committed to their next level will never be committed to yours. So, thank God for whatever good any of these people did in your life and quietly move on.

Successful relationships are the product of foundation, not heritage. So, someone can share your same background, but not your same best interest.

Remember: Nostalgia is about feelings produced by going backwards. That is not a problem when you just want to remember a fun vacation. But relationship disorder is only fixed in the realm of foundation not feelings.

Which is why in unhealthy relationships you only produce misery by how much energy is used trying to fix feelings instead of a faulty foundation.

➤ *Rate relationships by where you can and cannot go with them, and not by familiarity or family tree.*

➤ *Stay out of the whole, "but if you cannot trust family or friends then who can you trust" trap.* You trust those who value integrity more than familiar position.

➤ *Cut necessary strings for growth reasons, not drama ones.* Many times we do not take the plunge of making out of the box changes in our lives especially where relationships are concerned, until we have transformed what the situation is into a *Jerry Springer-esque* version of what the situation does not have to be.

In other words, we use drama to push us towards making decisions we are afraid to make without it.

My friend, Lourdes Hudson, said it to me like this one day: *"People, who are past their expiration date in your life are only there because of the strings they still have that keep them connected to you."*

We keep the strings because we fear the cold side of finality in something.

Realistically speaking, closing the door on an era of an expired us in anything messes with our fear of losing control more than any other area. So, human nature will leave more doors open just enough to soothe fear issues which in turn soothes control issues as well.

The problem is that most of these open doors end up accessing more eventual stress than reward. In that you are now carrying around so many parts of old you mixed with current you that you are too fragmented to be the best you.

Yes, finality does in fact have a cold side to it more than a sentimental one. But the cold side does not have to be an abusive or dramatic one. The cold is really the result of truth having no gray to it. It is black and white only. Which in turn forces our decisions to move on to be one color or the other.

2.

Avoid people who love the buzz of strife.

People who get a buzz over strife need strife in order to feed energy.

These are people who only perk up when there is controversy. The problem is that strife addicts are also destruction addicts who also thrive off of chaos in order to be noticed and heard.

This is one reason they stay in strife since they only have enough vision for the problems they can feed, not the ones they can solve.

It is not that strife addicts do not know truth, it is just that there is no buzz in the truth like there is in controversy.

Strife addicts are people who are enchanted with the problems of other people. The danger is that sooner or later your problems will enchant them enough too, so that your problems will be used against you.

Strife addicts are hurting people who resent how far in life their current acceptance of mediocrity will never be able to take them. So, rather than come up, they have to find whatever access they can to bring everyone else down. That is why their involvement in any relationship, any conversation, and any activity is from a judgmental, critical, manipulative, and dark perspective only. Finding the negative for them means finding agreement with their own darkness.

They never sustain anything good only because if everything stays good for too long, then there is not any room to derive excitement from experiencing damage.

➤ *Never complain over what you get from who, and what, you permit around you.*

What, or who, you permit to be the closest to you says everything about how much you value your dreams and goals. Anything you involve disorder, compromise, and greed in provides the proof of what you do not value.

➤ *Do not attempt to deal with strife sentimentally.*

The apostle Paul in the Bible equated strife to being cancerous. People who love drama cannot build anything. They can only bail themselves out of what they deteriorate or abuse. This is why you cannot deal with strife sentimentally.

This is not some issue of *"look at the beautiful tiger it's just a big pussycat."* Yeah right, as the big pussycat is chewing off your arm. Strife is destructive regardless of how well you know the parties involved.

➤ *Don't attempt to rationalize strife, much less negotiate with it.* Strife is not about who is wrong, but rather what is wrong. You can only expose it, reconcile it, or remove it. But you cannot play with it.

➤ *Don't personalize strife.* Strife is never personal. It is about a person's defiance of peace. Not their hatred for you.

Strife addicts are people unhappy with themselves and unhappy people only hate peace because they really hate how limited their fear makes them.

Where is your behavior or personal integrity off course with where you need to be in this area?

How would the person you want to be handle this area differently?

Leadership is never just about what you plan for. It is about what you adjust for.

6

YOU WILL SUCCEED BY WHAT IS PLANNED. YOU WILL GROW BY WHAT IS NOT.

Growth is what we adjust for, more than plan for.

So, while our success is determined by our ability to manage a plan, our strength is determined by our ability to manage what is unpredictable about a plan.

The average person does not fear change. They fear what the right adjustments will cost them and what they cannot control. Since obstacles are never scheduled, only conquered, with most obstacles your answers for moving around them never emerge until your decisions to shift gears to move around them does.

Meaning, you won't just get a plan to move around something tough; you will make a decision to not stay stuck, idle, or paralyzed and the plan, and eventually the necessary resources, will respond to your decision.

CEO FACT:

Any obstacle not permitted to enlarge your insight will only become the memorial to what sinks you.

We are only as helpless in any situation as we are helpless in what we think about the situation. Anything we cannot move around, we allow to beat us. So it's not a goal that separates us from others. It is how we deal with the obstacles to our goal that does. So if a superior goal does not consume us, a superior letdown will.

This is because we get stuck because of what is unpredictable. But we stay stuck because of what is unexplainable. Meaning, goals or obstacles bigger than what we currently are only require adjustments bigger than what we have currently made to deal with them.

CEO FACT:

Victory is the only mastery of adjustment.

Success does not respond to adrenaline. It responds to resolve. Which is why more compulsive and less productive prone people are more married to how a goal makes them feel than what a goal requires.

It's like this. The most productive time of a football game for a team accustomed to losing is before the game.

Why? Because of what they believe. That is where they at least have the hope that today might be their day. None of their game plan has been tested yet to see which parts of it will not work in reality. They are juiced on the adrenaline alone of how many things they have practiced for that should work. Of course, there is nothing wrong with the power of positive motivation.

However the most productive time of the game for the team accustomed to winning is usually half-time.

Why? Because of what they adjust. Winning teams are not just comprised of winning players, but also winning changes. Yes, they have the adrenaline too, but it does not matter which part of their plans before the game are not working in the game. They adjust to their desired end result. *Progress in anything will begin with what you are willing to sacrifice and end with what you are not. So, it is only how much you will give to any goal that says what you believe about it or not.*

It is not that losing teams cannot adjust . . . it's just that you cannot adjust to fix good intention. You can only adjust to meet a desired end result. So somewhere in the game, winning teams have to play by their resolve to win and not their adrenaline to win.

Which is one reason why *your method is what will inspire you, but your end result will be what drives you. Your only problem will be refusing to alter your method in order to reach your end result.*

Losing teams ask, "Why?" Winning teams ask, "How?" Winning teams do not need to be leading at halftime in order to be leading at the end.

And it is not that losing teams necessarily practice or prepare less than winning teams, it's just that they often times adjust slower.

CEO FACT:

Small thinkers never leave big ruts.

A mountain does not beat us. Our narrow perspective about a mountain beats us.

Rejection does not beat us. Our fearful perspective of rejection beats us.

Bad decisions do not beat us. Our dysfunctional loyalty towards a bad decision beats us. *Any obstacle that refuses to go away is just an indication of something big enough that we are not doing yet to resolve it.*

This is why often times our greatest delays are not because our obstacles are too big, but because our script for how we see our obstacles perfectly being conquered is too narrow.

It's like this: *Change is not about being good at it. It is rather about not being good at deteriorating and being lost. It is where you are lost that you will manage helplessness. Where you manage helplessness you will also manage depression.*

And you will not manage helplessness because you can't fight. You will manage helplessness because you resent where the fight is demanding more from you than you believe you should have to give.

CEO FACT:

Excuses are the babysitter for the unproductive.

Excuses are the fruit of blame. Blame is just the fruit of the refusal to take responsibility and adjust.

It is where you are protecting excuses that you are also protecting lack. Meaning, something good that you are supposed to have that the lies you may be protecting are incapable of giving you. Which also means you will always possess enough of something to upgrade anything that you have to a greater level as long as you are not using an excuse to keep it where it's at.

It's just that where you insist on inventorying what you lack, you will always blame what you have as being insufficient.

Excuses are what people make when they are controlled more by the fear of being wrong than they are the reality of staying limited. They are also what people make when they want to defend something that they do not want to grow in.

So, truth be told, we never just make excuses; we employ them to guard what we are trying to avoid instead of change.

Which is why *defeat is never about having pitfalls. It is about having no plan to move beyond good intentions.* So you will only use an excuse until failure or loss makes it impossible to.

What makes excuses deceptive is they function by reason. Meaning, our most unfulfilled and unproductive parts are only maintained because of how much we continually reason with them to stay that way.

1.

Make adjustments quickly.

The boardroom is where you will decide how much you would like to pay for your dreams. The battlefield is where you will discover just how much your dreams will cost you.

In the boardroom our reality of battle is optimistic. On the battlefield our reality of battle is corrected.

In the boardroom we make plans to win based on the vision we have. But on the battlefield we only win based on the vision we are willing to expand.

One reason is because inspiration only reveals which parts of a plan are possible. Not believable. Movement is what reveals what is believable.

➤ *Don't become enchanted with setbacks.*

Setbacks do not immobilize us because they can, but because we either become overwhelmed or enchanted by them. Overwhelmed meaning, most days there is not a difference between a good plan versus a bad one. There is only the presence of sobriety or the lack of it.

Enchanted meaning, where our identity is now derived from painting our mess-ups as *"so special"* that we actually feel more unique about them than convicted.

In other words, *"My screwup wasn't normal. Mine had lots of special parts to it that most other people's screwups never do."*

➤ *Get over the fact that you fell down and get over the fact that you miscalculated.* Accept that some days you will have to stumble just to discover something about your enemies that you could not see and something about your weaknesses that you were not dealing with.

2.

Get over disappointments quickly.

What is disappointment? *When your reality of something is not reality.*

Disappointment is when you thought something should work . . . not when reality said it would.

So, often times disappointment is just you asking deception to show you a picture of the way you think things should be because you resent where reality keeps showing you where they really are.

➤ *Don't lie to yourself about reality.* Reality does not lie to us. We lie to ourselves about reality. Problems do not lie to us. We lie to ourselves about our problems.

So, people stay paralyzed by disappointment because of what they have not repaired about their own lack of insight.

What will stop you from moving around disappointment? *Stubbornness.* Stubbornness is when we idolize our own version of reality or our own self-inclusive version of the truth too much.

➤ *There are only two kinds of people in the world—those who avoid challenges, and those who use challenges to obtain everything that those who avoid them complain about never having. Which one are you?*

3.

There will always be more than one stream that will lead to an ocean. Your only problem will be refusing to change streams to get there.

It is not until an obstacle births the wisdom for movement that it ceases to be an obstacle.

Champions shift gears. Losers shift blame.

So the average person will not blame because they lack answers more than they will blame because of what the answers will not permit them to function as.

➤ *Don't blame.* Blame in anything only helps you silence resentment. It does not silence reality.

So, the longer it takes for you to shift gears around an obstacle, the more an obstacle will consume you.

And since all change begins with something you currently have in you, people or resources do not have to get in line for your own improvements to begin.

➤ *Don't justify procrastination.* Where you have an excuse problem you will also have a procrastination problem that is fueling a denial problem. Improvements are never born out of denial.

Where is your behavior or personal integrity off course with where you need to be in this area?

How would the person you want to be handle this area differently?

Leadership is the ability to lead in spite of an enemy, not without one.

7

ADVERSITY WILL NOT DETERMINE WHO YOU ARE . . . IT WILL DETERMINE WHERE YOU WILL OR WILL NOT STOP. WHERE YOU WILL OR WILL NOT STOP WILL DETERMINE WHO YOU ARE.

We are not defined by our battles, only by our conduct in our battles. This is because it is never anything in our conflicts that stop us. It is only the leaders we choose not to be in our conflicts that does.

For that reason you cannot be the victim and the champion all at the same time, so with winning, it is never an issue of developing a deeper threshold for battle, but rather a deeper threshold for victory.

CEO FACT:

Achieving personal success is never about having battles we can manage. It is about having certain non-negotiables that can manage who we are in our battles.

Non-negotiables are steel. Steel is what the construction industry calls *"rebar."* Rebar is the internal steel that runs through the center of something to support what it is purposed to be. You can see it if you drive by a bridge or tall structure of some kind being constructed.

But when the construction is complete, you cannot see it. *You can only see the greatness it supports.*

It is only visible through everything great like a Golden Gate Bridge or Sears Tower in Chicago that is housed on it.

What is your rebar? The principles of internal steel comprised of functional and moral convictions and practices that center and enable you to carry what you are purposed to be. It's just that when your life is not built to carry what you are purposed to be, you will be left to manage everything you are not.

It's why some marriages refuse to collapse in tough times. Or some leaders refuse to take the easy way out even in the midst of controversy. Or a New York City refuses to cave in due to the aftermath of a 9/11 terrorist attack.

They are the principles and virtues that are in no way an issue of negotiation that you will not hesitate to enforce, rely on, and defend yourself by.

However, this is also where collapses happen—*when the weight of what something is purposed to be cannot be supported by the lack of what it currently is.*

Meaning, collapses happen where we are purposed to succeed, but are carrying the weight of too many issues that cannot be sustained by the places in us where we lack the steel of identity, character, and healthy esteem, much less a game plan for greatness.

Fear is what exploits our lack of internal steel in order for us to participate in everything mediocre, abusive, or chaotic that we resent going along with, but do not have enough internal character not to.

Rebar manages weight, and where we carry unnecessary emotional weight is through the fear and the anger of unresolved pain. However, rebar is for the purpose of carrying growth weight and productivity weight. It is not made to carry unresolved pain weight and immaturity weight, which is what fear and anger facilitates.

Fear is what tells us the types of things that we have to carry, and if we don't, *"then how are they going to get fixed, or who else is going to carry them?"*

So one of the great insecurities of human nature lies in how many people want to derive their worth, and their uniqueness, from how much weight in certain areas they can carry. It's like, *"I'm a strong person because I can pull truckloads of pain, fear, and dysfunction around every day."* And the moment that any of us assumes that it takes strength to manage disorder we will only keep managing bigger or longer doses of it until it kills us.

Three things happen when we lack steel in an area.

First, we live with faulty behavior because of the fear of rejection and failure which is really just the fear of success.

Secondly, we live with weak and destructive coping skills because there can never be steel enforced where there is unresolved pain. Steel can only support what is healthy, not what is sick. Hardness is what carries pain. Hardness is not strength. Hardness is just the wall around weakness.

Thirdly, we are left to depend on everyone else who has more steel than us.

Now you may say that this third issue is not such a bad problem since we all have to depend at various times in life on other people's strengths. However, our greatest limitations are never conquered because of the steel that someone else possesses. They are only conquered by the steel that we are willing to develop.

I mean let's face it. Someone else cannot go to the gym and work out, and you lose the weight. Their workout benefits their body. Your workouts benefit your body.

Someone else's steel can only help develop your steel, but their steel cannot support your high-rise.

CEO FACT:

No conflict can control you until it can use the unhealthy parts of you to manage the unhealthy parts of your conflict.

Most people do not find it easy to quit in a conflict because of the size of their battle. They quit because of how much who and what they are pledging their loyalties toward that cannot produce a victory in their conflict. Meaning, *all conflict enters your life because of the person you are. It is only conquered because of the person you are willing to become.*

So, where you lack self-respect, you will lack endurance. Where you lack the humility to be taught, rather than just affirmed, you will also lack wisdom.

Where you possess few healthy boundaries, you will also possess little internal strength.

The size of the conflict is never what does us in. The size of our unawareness does. So, it takes seeing something about yourself in order to see any of your unhealthy approaches to fighting. And while everyone in conflict gets hurt, only champions refuse to quit until they get something greater out of it than just their wounds.

CEO FACT:

Nothing unhealthy in us works alone.

This kind of bristles the average person upon hearing it. But there is a reality concerning where the most deficient parts of us gain a greater leverage to function more deficiently which is—*none of us participate with what is sick (unhealthy) unless there is something already sick in us.*

No, we are not just a bunch of twisted people. But nothing unhealthy in us works alone. Meaning, we are never just pulled along at gunpoint into what is insane, abusive, or destructive. We participate either because we were trained to, we are afraid not to, or we want to.

This is where we have to inventory the parts of us that manage sickness. Playing with sickness just allows us to stay sick.

So often times the legitimacy of our personal vision for success is only evident in the type of games that we no longer have time to play. Meaning, *people who are stuck in life are not often stuck in their limitations. Rather, they are stuck in their games. That is because a rut is not a rut because it can hold you. It is only a rut because of the games you play to stay in it.*

That is what games do; *they take the place of personal vision we do not have.* Which is why when you see a person who lacks boundaries in an area, they are suffering from a vision problem first.

Meaning none of us can even remotely say that we are ready for prosperity in something until we can steer our priorities and our lifestyle in a direction opposite of the games that we keep playing with everything that cannot prosper us.

Sickness attracts sickness. Health attracts health.

In 1979 when a Protestant fundamental preacher named Jim Jones led over eight hundred followers to mass death through drinking poisonous Kool-aid in a place called Jonestown, Guyana we immediately said, *"What a deranged maniac."* The next thing we said was, *"Who would follow such a leader?"* The answer was simple: *people just as sick as Jim Jones.*

But as sick as Jim Jones was at that point in his life, eight hundred people only listened to him as their leader because of what was just as sick in them. This is because *sick people only follow sick people.* Or to say it a different way, *we live and die based on what other people enable in us.*

Sick people do not make us do bad things. But they enable us to do bad things. So, on the doorstep of any personal growth you will have to decide what you are going to stop using in other people who make it easier for you to stay weak in specific areas.

For example, when parishioners come to me from what they consider to be an abusive church environment somewhere else, my counsel to them is never based on how bad their former pastor might have been to them. My counsel is always, *"What attracted you to that kind of church in the first place, and then, what was it in you that kept you there for so long?"* The abusive former pastor was just making it easier for the victimized parishioners to stay passive and void of personal integrity.

This is the law of Genesis; *one cannot multiply. It takes two.* I watch this in couples where either the man or the woman in the relationship has done something repeatedly perverted, violent, or immoral in the relationship. The first question everyone asks is, *"What did he/she see in that woman/man?"* Or, *"Why did he/she ever agree to marry them?"* That answer is just as simple too; *they were attracted by mutual sickness and bound by the same mutual sickness.*

Sick relationships can assuredly turn well because we are all living testimonies of that in different ways. But make no mistake. *There are never any victims of a sick relationship except children. Adults are willing participants not victims. They are volunteers of coexistence in the attempt to out-control and outmaneuver the other person's sickness.*

So the bottom line is none of us can change anything disorderly that we keep participating in. So when two people are sick together, it is absolutely irrelevant who has caused the most damage in the relationship.

And none of us get continually abused because someone else is abusive. Anything abusive that happens more than once only happens because something in us cooperates for it to.

A control freak cannot work unless there is a codependent to cooperate. A dominating person cannot work unless there is a passive, ultra-needy person too terrified of rejection or loss to play along.

And where do we identify the areas we are sick in? We can only recognize what is healthy or sick in our lives by its fruit. Unhealthy priorities and unhealthy paradigms never produce healthy results.

"But what if you don't know any better?" A lot of days we don't. But tragically this is where a person will stay sick; *where they insist that they can argue against their own worst fruit.* We can't. It is always the fruit of our behavior, our attitudes, and our decisions that showcases the real us despite how much effort we make to window dress an alternative us.

CEO FACT:

You will never possess the strength for going forward until going backwards is not an option.

Any victory in any battle comes down to improving the kinds of things you are good at. Some people shut down . . . other people step up. Whatever we are good at, we will act out on.

So when going backwards when the heat is on is predominantly what a person is good at, two primary reasons are to blame.

1. *In reality they were looking for a place to check out without looking bad. Their exit strategy was being planned for some time. This is because people who are good at avoiding and running only manage escape routes; they do not manage personal growth.*

2. *Going backwards is most comfortable, since going backwards never asks any questions, their coping skills are built around doing just that.*

This is why *you will only recognize personal growth when you keep coming to the same opportunities to go backwards, but you can't and won't.*

Most days in conflict the ruthlessness for going forward never kicks in until the ruthlessness against going backwards does. So, the drive to conquer any giant is merely a reality containing two elements.

1. Where a person will draw the line at how much they will minimize the amount of time they devote to sliding backwards.

2. How quickly they will slam on the brakes and kick things into overdrive to get back on track.

1.

To bounce back in anything you will have to know the difference between being tough and being hard.

Getting tough is about winning something, not proving something. Getting tough is about managing change. Getting hard is just about managing pain.

Being hard means you become bitter at tough times. Being tough means you become determined to get bigger than tough times.

And it's not that tough people have less stress, they just have less excuses for allowing inconvenience to keep them from getting something better than their disappointments.

➤ *Do not make permanent decisions in temporary situations.* Desperate decisions are what we make when we treat what is temporary as though it were permanent.

Remember: *anything that overwhelms you is just the proof of how much of the big picture you are currently not seeing.*

Pain only knows how to exploit what you do not presently understand. So, enlist the help of unbiased people who can challenge your perspective before you act out on it.

Besides, you will know wrong decisions because they are only made from a corner. Clarity does not place us in corners. Fear does.

➤ *Look at repetitive setbacks.* In other words, where you keep experiencing the same setbacks or the same type of destructive situations. They may be in different places, but they are all for the same reasons.

We only keep repeating the same dysfunctional cycles because we keep telling ourselves that we are in the same old traps but for new reasons.

➤ *Lessen the time that you devote to a rut.* To define frustration, it is nothing more than the presence of drive without the presence of insight.

So, frustration is never because of a rut you are in, but rather a rut you refuse to learn something to leave.

Ruts never just spit us out either. We either use the power of a restructured game plan and refocused energy to climb out of them or we stay in them long enough to learn how to manage them.

2.

Sow your losses as a seed.

I was having dinner one evening with renowned preacher, Dr. Oral Roberts, and his now deceased wife, Evelyn.

I was eager to ask a man of his stature about his secrets of how he had walked through tough times over the years of his high-profile ministry.

In his explanation he made this statement to me. *"I learned to sow my losses as a seed."* That was all that he said on that topic.

It was not until later that evening that the real impact of what this meant really hit me—*my failures only glory in anything paralyzing that I cannot let go of. They fear anything I can.*

This is in part the myth about what we know as *"just getting over something."* You and I just can't get over deep and traumatic painful things. We either outgrow them or we develop coping skills and paradigms to coexist with them. But we never just get over them.

Everybody loses. And none of us are ever big enough for where we want to be until we agree to become bigger than what we have lost. Which would explain why the secret to success is multiplication, not replacement.

Granted, somewhere along the way we have all lost a piece of our heart or our dream. But that is where we change what we've lost by choosing to work towards what is new.

We only work towards depression when we work towards what is the same. And we only stay neutralized by what we keep living to replace. But the best of tomorrow never births until you are through trying to put back the worst parts of yesterday.

So, how do you become a better sower than collector?

First, when you sow your losses as a seed, you disarm your limitations from being able to hold against you what you now refuse to hold against yourself.

In other words, what you will not release, you will relive. So, your enemy can only hold against you what you insist on holding against yourself.

A failed relationship, or career, a loved one gone . . . processing reality is one thing. Deciding to deteriorate is another. So, while you cannot fix yesterday regardless of how much of it was or was not your fault, you can fix how much of yesterday you will not repeat tomorrow.

Secondly, when you sow your losses as a seed, you disarm your enemy from being able to brag that he stole something. When loss stays absorbed, it stays a loss.

All absorbing drains. But when loss is released it becomes a seed that grows to produce the harvest of something greater.

So to conquer negative absorbing *you cannot wait to release things until after you can explain them.*

Meaning personal victory begins and ends where your faith does, not where your answers do. So, starting over is not about the fact that we may be hurting. It is about the fact that we have nothing to lose. It is only when we refuse to start over that loss has beaten us.

➤ *Don't wait for the magic carpet ride out of pain.* Stop being the baseball team looking for the one grand slam to win the game. Stop being the boxer looking for the one big punch to end the fight. Growing bigger than loss is a process that you will have more than one bad day of.

That's okay. Just keep pulling yourself together and keep moving in a forward direction, even on the days when your steps are smaller.

➤ *Learn your way past pain. Don't willpower your way past it.* Pain can only stay where we are in the dark about something. It must leave where there is light.

So, moving on in anything always surrounds the entrance of insight. Insight is what sustains fortitude.

On the days when you just have to suck it up in the dark . . . great. But you cannot run by stuffing. You can only run by releasing. And nothing painful is ever released until it can be released through something you have learned.

➤ *Choose faith more than logic.*
Faith will grow you. Whereas logic will just tick you off.

Logic only helps you explain yesterday until you have so many reasons for why yesterday existed, you are too depressed and enraged to grow past anything.

Faith however rebuilds today. Faith also involves forgiveness. It's just that faith is much harder because we have to trust that tomorrow can be different with few positive reference points to guarantee it.

3.

No one has to like you in order for you to start over.

Enough said.

Where is your behavior or personal integrity off course with where you need to be in this area?

How would the person you want to be handle this area differently?

Leadership is the ability to shift gears, not blame.

8

IT'S NOT WHAT KNOCKS YOU DOWN THAT CHANGES YOU. IT'S WHAT MAKES YOU GET BACK UP THAT DOES.

Nothing about falling down ever changes our lives; it can't. If messing up could change our lives, we would become too perfect to mess up. The change comes in the comeback.

Why? Because of all that we have to become differently to get back up, compared to who we just had to be to fall down. *We only get back up in anything when we are willing to do something different than what we did to fall.*

And the reality is that most people live their lives trying not to fall instead of living their lives trying not to be mediocre.

CEO FACT:

Talented people do not bounce back. Driven people do. So, wherever you quit is all that your limitations ever have to pay for your next seasons of greatness.

When this price is paid, it can feel like a load has just been lifted off of our shoulders. The load of responsibility and vulnerability that goes into all change.

However, the level we are on presently only works until it is time to grow further. Then everything that has previously been permissible for us to tolerate, and even succeed in, on this present level now becomes what divides us, exhausts us, and ultimately derails us if we do not upgrade the rules for winning the game.

Remember: *Failure is not what beats us. Passivity does.* Which means you and I are only as good as the amount of time that it takes for us to apply the changes from greater truth and rebound from the disappointments of self-deception.

And when it comes to understanding why some people quit, people do not just quit on their dreams and goals. They shut down on where their dreams and goals were demanding more growth out of them than they wanted to pay. That is what quitting is—*shutting down.*

So fear will negotiate with our limitations to purchase the pieces of purpose and potential that our vulnerability tells us will cost too much in overcoming personal limitations to reach. All by offering us places to settle on this side of sacrifice if we will trade being prosperous for being safe. That is what managing mediocrity is. Managing the things that are familiar in order to manage a place of safety.

CEO FACT:

Character is not what you get when you hit the wall. Rather, it's what you build before the wall that allows you to avoid the wall all together.

It's like this; you will either own your purpose or own your traps, but never both. So, with repeated setbacks they are simply the proof that our traps own more of us than we own of ourselves.

You know what a trap is, right? The places where the greatest unmet needs and the biggest unhealed deficiencies position us to experience the most unnecessary losses.

This is because to live as a victim of a trap, it requires us to give away our power of ownership to the trap for the trap to have power. Meaning, no trap works just because it is a trap. They only work as long as our fear or lazy character empowers them to be traps for us.

However, this is the great deception when it comes to the chaotic aspect of failure that we call *"hitting the wall."* The assumption is that somehow after hitting the wall is when we make our most effective changes as a result of the temporary sobriety that the wall provokes in us. Not so.

Yes, we do feel our most sober at these moments, but that is mostly due to all of the guilt that we are now feeling that has silenced the realm of fantasy and self-deception that we were functioning by just before the crash.

Character is a process. Not a collision. Character is not what we build after a crash. Rather, it is what we build after we decide that we are going to stop doing the things that wreck us.

And we do not develop this character when we are caught. We develop it after the dust has settled from our crashes and we decide if we are sick enough yet at how much of life we are losing by never outgrowing the same setbacks.

This is because the wall cannot change us. *It can only take advantage of where we are not changing.* Which is why a huge deception that so many people live by is the assumption that because the wall got their attention, it must have fixed their problems too. Not exactly. The wall just wakes us up. It puts us in the *"I see"* mode. It does not put us in the *"I change"* mode. What we do while we are awake is a completely different issue.

"Yes, but one day I hit rock bottom and that really jolted me into making the kinds of changes I needed to make, and I have never hit bottom again." Not exactly that way either.

I'm sure that is what it feels like when it happens for some of us. However, hitting anything hard is never what finally changes us. It is when we get sick and tired of losing that does.

Getting sick and tired enough of everything that you are supposed to have, but constantly keep living without, is a conviction that can turn you around even without a crash involved. It's just that the average person will wait for the crash to help them finally submit to the conviction.

So, most people will keep hitting the wall simply because they only recognize the pain of a mistake, more than they recognize the opportunity to stop making one. That is not insight. That is delusion.

So while hitting the wall the first time can be the result of ignorance, hitting the wall the second time will only be the result of indifference.

We only hit walls because of all the warning signs that we choose to ignore on our way there. The signs reveal the traps.

So, a little insider information *(don't tell Martha Stewart)*: *where you want to stop messing up, make the signs your new best friend.*

It's like this: the same setbacks always come with the same potholes. That is where indifference comes in. *Indifference is the self-preserving disregard for anything good that can save us from a lot of everything bad. Meaning where a hardness of heart has permitted prideful arrogance to convince us that we can survive the long-term effect of playing games with what is broken, fraudulent, or deficient.*

So when we crash, it is never because we did not see the signs. It's just that we did not care enough when we did. That is how indifference develops. So, at the end of the day the wall does not make us smart. *It makes us caught.*

And while the wall can definitely make us repentant, it does not make us different. A different us is only the result of what we do differently with the same destructive signs the next time that we notice them.

CEO FACT:

Avoiding the wall means restructuring our boundaries. To restructure our boundaries we will have to restructure our tolerance of pain that being too dysfunctional for too long has made us immune to handle. Which is one reason we keep hitting the wall.

Jungle trackers will allow themselves to get bit with poisonous reptiles or insects multiple times as a way of building immunity against the poison.

However, this principle does not work so well when it comes to self-destruction. People will only continue to hit the wall because of what their tolerance for the pain and destruction of the wall has developed in them.

So, people become immune to loss until there is nothing more they can lose. They become immune to aborting good jobs, good relationships, and good opportunities until they can be no more alone and any deeper in lack. So on a chaos scale of one to ten, they do not even wake up to smell the chaos coffee until it is already at a nine.

They become immune to abusive relationships until there is just no more hope or esteem left to see themselves with any other kind of people.

One reason these type of people do this is because of what they are not making adjustments about in between visits to the wall. About the only thing that they are doing is medicating their level of denial of all the reasons why they keep hitting one.

Avoiding a wall is only possible by the adjustments we make after the last time we hit it. So, we will only hit the wall the second time because of the lies we tell ourselves about the wall after the first time we hit it.

Do not expect the wall to stop being the wall in order for you to stop hitting it. *We only stop hitting walls because we change, not because the walls do.*

So, what do you do? First of all, stop waiting for the wall. It's only the people who are waiting for crisis to bring them to reality that in reality are doing more to cope with the pain of crisis than they are changing the reasons for a crisis.

Secondly, self-deception is the first step towards deterioration. It is not great maturity when you only notice the trap once you're in it.

The Secret Service does not get paid to recognize a would-be assassin after he/she has shot at the president. They get paid to notice before.

Avoiding the wall means restructuring your boundaries. In order to restructure your boundaries, you will have to restructure your tolerance of pain that your dysfunction has made you immune to handle without having the right boundaries.

Thirdly, anytime you protect negative compromise you will have to use manipulation to do it. Which in reality means you become the biggest liar you have ever experienced.

Lastly, you cannot wait to put up proper boundaries at the end of something and expect things to be different at the beginning. Change never occurs in anything that you are cleaning up after the fact.

CEO FACT:

You will have to be going after something big in order to get over something bad.

Big goals are the only things that pull us past bad yesterdays. So, a setback bigger than you have ever had only requires a plan bigger than you have ever had to get over it.

People only decide what they cannot overcome because they decide where it is okay not to grow any further. So while falling down can be a result of what you did not see, how long you stay down will only be the result of what you did not fix.

CEO FACT:

How you get back up will determine how you live the rest of your life.

None of us ever just learn leadership. We learn instead where we will or will not move past obstacles, setbacks, and fear and then that is what determines our leadership.

So, comebacks are never fueled by what happens to your enemy, but rather, by what happens to your understanding. Understanding is the beginning of knowledge, not the beginning of revenge.

The purpose of recovery is greater effectiveness, not greater popularity. So, you can get back up bitterly, but your future will just be comprised of using yesterday's pain to make today's opportunities pay.

It's like this: God gives every leader the same chance to land on their feet. It's just that some refuse to stand up. So, in growing in leadership, it does not change our battles, it changes our responses. Our different responses change our battles.

Change for the better in anything is the only proof that you have won the battle.

1.

Wherever a stronger part of you is demanding to live, a weaker part of you will have to die.

You will only stay connected to something unhealthy because of how you see it and not because of what it is. Meaning, fear tells you, you are trapped because fear can only work through a limited or unhealthy perspective of anything.

➤ *Don't try to resent your way out of anything undesirable.* None of us leave where we are or what we are because we resent it. Insight is the only way that we move on from anything. So, unless you leave a void of maturity in something, then just being able to leave a bad situation does not help you.

Insight is not the accruement of truth . . . it is the application of truth.

2.

You are never losing where you are learning.

Failure can never take anything from you until your own arrogance and indifference says it can. So, learning is what disarms your setbacks from being able to be held against you.

If time and space could change us, then the sacrifice to learn in the midst of pain or miscalculation would be unnecessary.

We could just wait out the pain. However, you cannot replace loss. You can only fix why you lose. You cannot replace what is gone. You can only change how you will manage what you obtain about tomorrow differently.

3.

You will only get back up by solving a personal defect, not a situation.

You cannot change a negative situation; you can only change who you are in a negative situation.

People who only try to change situations end up changing scenery more than defects.

This is also why the average person falls down and immediately wants to repair everyone else's perception of his/her fall. That does not solve anything.

You cannot want to get back up on the horse so fast that nothing is different about you the next time you fall off.

Where is your behavior or personal integrity off course with where you need to be in this area?

How would the person you want to be handle this area differently?

Leadership is not exhausting, mediocrity is.

9

YOU WILL ONLY ENTER WHERE YOU WANT TO BE WHEN YOU ARE AT THE TOP OF WHERE YOU ARE.

You will never leave a season of life or an undesirable situation until your own personal progress makes you overqualified to be there.

This is because none of us just move on in something simply because we feel ready or because we are hurt or disgusted. We move on because we are no longer the same people we were when we only qualified to be where we are. Meaning it is only our personal growth in anything that places movement to any situation that our lack of growth has been holding us in.

Remember. Growth always produces its own distance. So, welcome to the great hypocrisy of human nature—*when we want something better out of life than the individuals we are willing to become to get it.*

You see, people just don't improve because they want to be good and decent. They improve because of everything that is not good and decent that they no longer want to participate in.

This is because *we do not get what we want. We get what we are willing to position our growth to obtain.*

So, the quality of our lives is only proportionate to the level we are on as people. And if we want to upgrade life quality then we must upgrade personal quality first.

CEO FACT:

You will only move on from what you are overqualified for.

No one ever just stays the same when it is time to change levels. They either change something in order to move forward or they go backwards just to be able to fit back in with where they've been. But no one ever just stays the same.

The past does not leave us until we can outgrow it.

Childhood abuse does not leave us until we can outgrow it.

The weight of betrayal, divorce, or abandonment does not leave us until we outgrow it.

Heck, forgiveness towards your most negative circumstances is even impossible until a piece of your own personal growth has changed your perspective enough and made it releasable. *Personal pain only gets smaller when personal growth flourishes bigger.*

That is what growth is. It is not hating our way to progress or twelve stepping our way. It is first removing how much fear, pride, and denial we are using to absorb pain and disappointment. Then it is removing how many lies we are embracing that justify where our current limitations cannot produce the end results that we are supposed to have. Then it is removing the excuses we are making to stay more presumptuous or hurt than insightful.

This is not some graduation with attitude of, *"You'll see. You'll all be sorry you doubted me. . . ."* Of course, while the song, *"I Will Survive"* plays in the background. It is rather the disarming of who, and what, has the ability to stop you dead in your tracks on any given day, by using your own growth to do the disarming.

It's like this: *Life is not about a cure. It is about using your own growth to not permit the disease from problems to be in your center.*

So, centeredness, or what people often refer to as *"finding their center,"* is not a state of mind. It is a state of priority. It is an arrangement of our lives around how much purposed fulfillment we are permitting ourselves to live with or without.

Which is why unnecessary emotional weight, or *"emotional obesity"* as I refer to it in my next book project, is never the presence of unfulfillment. Rather, it is the acceptance of unfulfillment.

And none of us ever just arrive at being centered until we make decisions to stop controlling the things that keep us so out of balance.

CEO FACT:

Part of removing chaos will be removing what is in you that attracts it.

Most people only complain about chaos. They seldom analyze why it keeps finding them.

Chaos does not enter your life because it wants to, but because it has a place to fit. And chaos only fits inside of the broken and deficient parts of us.

I mean let's face it, the same destructive patterns do not just repeat themselves because you happen to be one of those *"bad things that keep happening to good people"* persons. Your destructive parts keep setting up the dominoes for the destructive patterns to keep knocking them down.

So, the average leader assumes that they can get rid of disorder by getting rid of disorderly people. It is way easier for the average leader to blame who or what is there than it is to deal with how it got there.

Why? Because blame assists denial. So where denial enters your company, your relationships, your marriage, your parenting, your finances, or your personal life, it has to go through your own mediocrity to do it.

Mediocrity is where a leader has lazy character. Lazy character is where a leader permits disorder. Disorder is what kills leaders, and anything unproductive you can fit in with, you cannot change.

So, you cannot use denial to maintain peace and then call that a humble solution.

The tragedy, however, of much of mainstream society is in how many people are not trying to change to fulfill a destiny. They are just trying to distance themselves from fear or pain. They will change scenery before they will change a personal defect in order to do it.

Which is why people in the middle of the road are not necessarily people without a side. Rather, they are people without the backbone to pick one.

Now mind you, a change of scenery at strategic times is not only very needed, but very productive. However, where you are avoiding a challenge to step up your game in an area, then the only scenery you will be looking for is the scenery that your defects will fit in better with. Then you will mistake what feels like safety as change.

CEO FACT:

The only mistake you will make in conquering tomorrow is assuming that tomorrow's giants will be the same as today's so your weaponry can stay the same also.

We never lose because our enemies get bigger, but because our battle techniques stay smaller.

This is what Barbara Tuchman showed in her book, *The Guns of August*. That one source of the early damage of World War I was largely due to the fact that both America and Russia had never bothered to change their approach from previous wars. Times had changed, but their weapons and their approach had not.

New beginnings are never possible with old behavior. So, wanting something great is only a problem when you are unwilling to make great changes to get it.

And the issue with making great changes is realizing that *finishers are not people with bigger thresholds for battle, but rather people with smaller thresholds for using outdated or unproductive battle techniques.*

Which will also be your only handicap with overcoming disappointments and miscalculation—

where you are experiencing new setbacks, but you are still processing them as the same old person.

CEO FACT:

Bigger rewards are only the result of removing bigger stumbling blocks.

You want bigger money? Solve bigger problems.

You want to solve bigger problems? Become a bigger person.

Anything greater than what you have will only be on the other side of the greater obstacles you will choose to remove to get it. And any obstacle only remains an obstacle as long as our limited perspective and ineffective approach tells them they can be.

This is what also helps define true success in your life. *Success is the result of taking on what the average are trying to avoid.* Meaning, most day's success will not be based on what you know. It will be based on what you are willing to take on. It is only an average leader who expects to be rewarded for position more than solutions.

You will fall because of what you lack. But you will bounce back because of what you have learned. So, while the decision to use an obstacle may be your enemy's, the decision to move around one will be yours.

Which also means you cannot place so much space between where you fall and where you get back up that you permit failure to take from you what a decisive vision and a functional identity would otherwise never let it have.

This would explain the two distinct realities when dealing with tough obstacles.

1. You don't change an obstacle; you change your approach to an obstacle. A different you can no longer be neutralized by the same things.

Most obstacles never start big; they become big when our limited coping skills give them size. For most obstacles they are usually only as big as what we make them in their beginning stages.

So, we are only considered improved people by what we no longer can be derailed by the same way.

2. Obstacles just don't go away when they are finished being obstacles. So, you will have to decide when an obstacle is finished being an obstacle for you.

And you will never decide this until you can decide how much loss is enough for you.

This is why fear is so powerful in that it can only fill the places of us where enough insight has not.

Fear shrinks our perspective of everything that the reality of a situation is by over-inflating everything that the reality of that situation is not.

So, most things that can feel like they are the end of the world are usually only the end of your personal vision and understanding. Since no obstacle is ever the end of the world except where your world is revolved around having that obstacle.

HOW TO CHANGE IT . . .

1.

What are the top three things you have been convicted to change on your present level, but still haven't?

1.________________________________

2.________________________________

3.________________________________

2.

What things can you identify about your present level that are either outdated or unproductive that you keep trying to negotiate to take with you to a new level?

1.________________________________

2.________________________________

3.________________________________

3.

Your decisions to succeed will only be as good as your changes to succeed.

You cannot achieve something significant by using something defective.

Winners first decide to win, and then they change to win before they ever practice to win.

Winners build their preparation around their changes. Whereas losers just build their preparation around their good intentions.

Like professional teams who have players being arrested in the off-season or showing up to training camp out of shape. They have not decided to win more than they are just assuming they will.

4.

You cannot begin to outgrow what you cannot begin to own.

Make a list of your realistic goals for removing debt, making purchases, and establishing a greater measure of ownership of your life in believable stages over the next twelve months.

Make a list of the areas of the personal you that currently do not function in ownership of yourself.

These are the areas where codependence, lack of boundaries, et cetera, reside.

Then decide what you are going to need to adjust about your habits, relationships, and lifestyle in order to fit your goals into the next twelve months. Of course, without losing your family, sanity, and your sense of movement in the process.

Remember: *anything you want will always begin with something in your present you are willing to trade to get it and end with something you are not.*

Where is your behavior or personal integrity off course with where you need to be in this area?

____

____

____

____

____

____

____

How would the person you want to be handle this area differently?

____

____

____

____

____

____

____

Leadership is never
determined by the number
of those who follow,
but rather the progress of
those who follow.

10

WHEREVER YOUR LEARNING STOPS, THEN SO WILL YOUR CAPACITY TO FACILITATE GREATNESS.

You and I are only as good as the level of teachers who speak into us and the level we allow them to speak on.

And at the foundation of learning *we will only learn to the level that we see ourselves going to.*

Meaning, we never change levels in life because we want to learn; *we learn because we want to change levels.*

One reason is because wisdom that only helps you stay on the level you are on is not wisdom. It might have been wisdom when it got you there, but if it is keeping you there it is self-protection. All wisdom contains movement to it, simply because it contains freedom with it also.

So all learning is tied to a destination that you want to be. And any place better that you do not see yourself going to, you will not connect with the kinds of insight and teachers who can take you there.

One reason is because every defect in your life will stem from a defect in your wisdom first. This is because incompetence in anything always begins with something we are taught and only ends with something we are taught. Meaning, most days the only reason we do dumb things is because our distorted sense of understanding tells us we can.

So the moment we position ourselves to embrace anything that can change us, it will cost us a paradigm we already believe and a habit we already facilitate.

CEO FACT:

Your problems with learning will cause a hang-up. Your problems with authority will maintain a hang-up.

People do not hate their hang-ups; *they hate accountability.* So, their problems never lie in the things they may do ineffectively, but rather in the things they refuse to learn to do differently from other people who do them better.

The accruement of education is determined by knowledge. But the deep insight that changes behavior, lifestyle, pain, et cetera, is only determined by trust.

Most days where our learning is deficient, it is because we have traded where we really need insight for where we will settle for just being educated simply so we can avoid trusting.

This problem with trust is not based on what we are afraid to see about our teachers. It is more what we are afraid that our teachers may see about us. So hang-ups are protected.

And before we go any further with this, let's understand one thing. *Deep learning never happens by personalizing or acting shocked concerning your deficient parts.*

People want to act shocked at where they could even be deficient and then wonder why they lack the transparency necessary to solve the problem.

This is where our worst hang-ups are inherited from—trying to follow unhealthy teachers and survive traumatic or perverted experiences.

This also defines what bad esteem is. Bad esteem is simply the acceptance of what everything abusive has said about us. Meaning, lies always surround abuse.

And the biggest lie that surrounds all abuse is the lie that we are only good enough to abuse. From this the typical brainwashing of *not good enough, not worthy, not valuable, not going to achieve a lot, never will have a lot, et cetera,* proceeds.

Abuse can tell us two things. Either we are not lovable because those abusing us do not love themselves. This is the *"you're only good enough to abuse"* form of abuse.

Or, we in fact are lovable but only after everyone else's needs have been satisfied. This is the *"we have to lose in order for someone else to win"* form of abuse. It's the good child of sorts that is trained to compensate for the bad adult.

This form of abuse can happen right smack dab in the middle of a middle class, prom queen, never been hit, sexually molested, or parents never divorced home.

So, our trained behavior is sculptured to believe wrong about ourselves just to fit in with what we feel powerless to change.

Hence, the existence of our hang-ups that become the memorials we have built to abusive encounters we have absorbed and problems we have refused to learn from and overcome. Which now through adulthood, act out as the coping skills for what has become our version of abused *(distorted)* truth.

That is what a hang-up is: *the protective mechanism we have developed to protect pain or a lie.*

The primary danger however is that over time, we learn to trust our hang-ups to dangerously dysfunctional levels. In that our whole functioning system for processing life on all its major fronts is built to manage limitations more than fulfillment.

This is because hang-ups never breed prosperity in anything.

One reason is because hang-ups protect comfort. They demand nothing from us much less correct anything about us.

So where any of us trust our hang-ups more than we should, we will also treat error as truth. Unhealthy things that should detest us, inappropriate things that should slap us with obvious reality, actually don't. They are treated like normal instead, or at the very least justified when we need to victimize from a position of when we were victims.

CEO FACT:

You cannot lead better than you follow.

This is the other frontier of lifelong learning besides the issue of overcoming hang-ups. The great perversion of leadership, *"Lead everyone, but follow no one."*

In life we reproduce what we are, not what we wished we were, and not what we tell other people to be.

So, you cannot take other people where you are not or teach others what you have never permitted someone else to teach you.

This is why self-taught people can be dangerous because of their assumption that they can recognize all of the answers they need without being able to recognize all of the problems they have.

Healing in everything comes through the relationships that God uses to bring a perspective to our weak or hurting parts that we either were incapable of seeing or did not want to. This is why self-taught people love being self-taught; they can pick and choose their own accountability to the truth.

Their logic for remaining mobile enough to protect isolation can be used when needed to justify what they do not want to see themselves as deficient in.

People embrace being self-taught in order to avoid having to trust. And none of us ever learn because we have problems. We only succeed with deep learning because we make ourselves vulnerable enough to truth to risk being misunderstood, judged, scorned, or even manipulated for even having problems.

This is why being self-taught also tempts you to validate your own blind spots too much. This is not an issue of not being self-educated or driven to learn on days when no qualified teachers are around. But people with authority problems also have pride problems.

In pride we use intellectualism. Not intellectualism for growth purposes, but more for minimizing reality purposes. With intellectualism we can protect our perspective of something much easier than enlarge it. We can create theories that say the things that we wish the fruit of the real us was really saying.

So obviously while intellectualism is not all bad, it is still not insight. It is only education.

Whereas learning is the submission to correction. Which creates freedom over the codependence that keeps us attached to the type of thinking and behavior that does more to demote personal power than establish it.

CEO FACT:

Your commitment to learning will have to mean more to you than the approval of inaccurate people.

When unprincipled people reject you, it is a favor.

When principled people reject you, it is a wake-up call. This is one reason why it would be better to be persecuted by someone with a lesser standard than alienated by someone with a higher one.

No, this does not mean turn into some judgmental stick in the mud. But it does mean that when error on some level does not grieve you it usually means you are in it. It is also highly dangerous if those around you know more error than you know truth, which makes their error appear reasonable. Besides, deceived people only like you because they can see a resemblance of themselves in you.

Just look at where more functional people who have what you are supposed to have cannot connect with you.

It's not that healthy people will not help you or be a part of your change process. It's just that they will not participate with you while you defend your right to be unhealthy by you describing your traps as being enchanting or unfixable and your unethical behavior as being part of your unique individuality.

1.

Don't be cheap with those whose wisdom has minimized the distance to your goal.

This is what great mentors and strategic teachers do; *they minimize the distance to your goals.* Meaning, one insight from what someone great has sacrificed to discover for themselves can potentially take years off of you having to bleed to discover it for yourself.

This brings up the issue of people who are cheap with their learning. No, not cheap with wanting to pay back school loans. But cheap with how they reward and pursue the level of teachers who have and can produce the greatest dividends in their life.

Cheap people are people who are stupid on purpose.

Cheap people are looking for a hand-out, instead of a solution. Learning is a price, not a gift. At no time can cost be compared to results.

So some days your answers are only as valuable as what you are willing to pay to obtain them.

➤ *If you will not pay for your most effective wisdom, you will not pay to apply it either.* It is only a parasite who wants for free what it has cost others everything to obtain. So your enemies only hope of succeeding against you is to convince you that being stubborn, cheap, or arrogant in the presence of another's expertise is actually a sign of individuality rather than downfall.

A cheap person is also a lazy person. What lazy people turn into are climbers. A climber is someone who wants everything and will defend nothing, while agreeing to pose as anything in order to get a piece of something.

2.

What do you do when your lack of character creates crisis or costs you something?

Do you get mad? Or do you get honest?

How comfortable are you fixing a problem in spite of who knows about it and what they may be saying?

Is perception more important than solution? Or is your idea of a solution only that which helps you maintain perception?

Remember: *Other people do not notice your flaws, they experience them.* So, it is perverted to assume that what you are okay with about your mediocre parts, others are as well.

3.

Don't ask someone to teach you what you will not document.

Wise teachers speak for answers more than trivia. So keep a note pad or a microcassette with you always.

What hits you in a moment could change you for a lifetime, but may not be remembered later.

Where is your behavior or personal integrity off course with where you need to be in this area?

How would the person you want to be handle this area differently?

Leadership is as much the hatred for disorder as it is the talent for order.

11

SUCCESS IS NEVER THE RESULT OF HARD WORK. IT IS THE RESULT OF EXCELLENCE. EXCELLENCE IS THE RESULT OF HARD WORK.

Prosperity responds to two things, excellence and purpose. Excellence is hard work in that it never allows you to settle. It always demands that you continually refine it.

This is where the average person accepts mediocrity in something as the alternative.

Excellence is not a gift. It is not a college course. There is only one element that produces it: *honesty.*

Honesty in that the average person tends to accept mediocrity only because they do not want to accept where their effort or end result needs improvement. They personalize instead every flaw in themselves that the effort to achieve excellence will expose.

Know this: *Excellence does not validate you. It rewards you.* So, achieving excellence in anything is only about being ruthless with yourself. It is never about being ruthless with a problem.

And since we have to facilitate mediocrity in order to have any, a tendency is to fall prey to the trap of needing our effort to validate us rather than pushing the envelope for excellence and having our excellent end result reward us.

For this reason excellent people will stop at their end result, whereas mediocre people will stop at their good intention.

CEO FACT:

You will never work hard enough to compensate for permitted mediocrity or excusable ignorance.

We don't work hard and become successful. We work hard and become excellent. Excellence is what makes us successful.

This is one reason why some leaders work hard but have nothing. *They are working hard to go nowhere.*

Personally I used to believe that success was the result of hard work until I realized one day that much of my hard work was being used to bail water from all the holes that my lack of excellence was creating. *Anyone can work hard. But not everyone can work hard to capitalize on excellence that they have. Many just work hard to compensate for the excellence they don't.*

So while everyone on the outside would look at the Konrad of old and label me as *"driven,"* which could be considered a compliment, my drive back in my old dysfunctional days was not being used to build anything great. It was just being used to replace everything disorderly I kept recycling.

You will always know where you lack excellence in your leadership because of how much effort you spend existing or replacing rather than growing and multiplying. It's kind of like if I am playing football, and I am running towards the wrong end zone, running faster does not help me.

Excellence is not about driving the Rolls Royce. It is about driving a clean Toyota. Excellence is not about having custom tailored clothing. It is about having an organized closet.

However, how a leader sets up his/her system of order or lack thereof, will say everything about what they would rather do with their resources.

Remember: *Damage control is not progress. Expansion and multiplication are.* Being able to survive fires is not the same as being able to build a fireproof system.

So, it is perverted to think that you can clean up your life, but you will not clean up your car, your closet, your checkbook, your appearance, et cetera.

CEO FACT:

You will have to learn order before you can learn leadership, or else your leadership will be known for its disorder.

Disorder is not about minding clutter. It is about not minding delays. People who applaud disorder also applaud no confrontation.

So while all leaders in fact deal with obstacles, its only uncommon leaders who will not use sloppiness to create unnecessary ones.

Just ask the uncommon employee who eventually gets promoted to the corner office, and they will tell you it was because of how orderly they kept the mailroom.

Ask the person who knows how to manage several thousand dollars, and they will tell you it is because of knowing how to manage minimum wage. *Excellence breathes an energy whereas disorder only consumes energy.*

So, when it comes to how far we go in life, we do not go as far as our skills can take us. We only go as far as our own disorder is not permitted to sabotage us.

I learned this lesson in particular by watching a minister colleague of mine who was always complaining about the continual crisis within his ministry where his employees were concerned.

He had even invited several well-known consultants in to trouble shoot his problems and tell him who the culprit was. However, the only problem was that he was the culprit.

This was because it was his own personal anger that permitted his standard for chaos. Chaos was how he could control.

But you would never know that based on how much he would complain about it not to mention intellectually explain all the ways it was not his fault.

It was simple. His weakness permitted his staff to function in their weakness, which could only in turn multiply the chaos. His constant anger was largely fueled by a poor standard he was refereeing that he refused to accept as his own poor standard. So he would just blame it on everyone else's.

Rather than changing his own standard, he would just keep hiring the kind of inferior employees that were too impressed with his presentation but could only reinforce his dysfunction. Then he could blame them.

Sometimes he would actually hire good people who were expected to outperform a faulty system and would sooner or later just burn down until they were too exhausted to be happy about what they were doing.

One way to know that we are in denial about our own mediocrity is how good we have become at defending it more than removing it.

The real tragedy of my friend's situation was that he had more excuses than changes. He could out argue just about everybody as to why he was continually repeating the same dysfunctional system.

That is one way that we know where we are refereeing disorder in something; *how articulate we have become in convincing ourselves and others about how much the same scenarios that we keep participating in are somehow all for a legitimate reason, and almost always a resource or circumstantial fault, before they are our fault.*

It's like this. Any of us can be as driven to maintain disorder as we can be to maintain growth. Even though my preacher friend was every talented and very driven, for any of us, our compromise will destroy anything that our talent can build.

CEO FACT:

Any part of your life that you have not prepared to succeed with order, you have prepared to fail with chaos.

Disorder is the result of what you permit.

Excellence is the result of what you enforce.

Order simply means, *"the accurate arrangement of things."* So, upgrading your standard in anything has nothing to do with something you are given, but rather something you are tired of.

So you will have to go after your disorder as passionately as you go after your dreams, or your disorder will cause your dreams to appear farther away than they really are.

That is what disorder is. It is not the lack of resources. It is the lack of integrity. And where any leader has a problem with disorder, they have a problem with accountability also.

Order creates energy. Disorder drains it. A lack of progress means a lack of oxygen. Any place you cannot recognize disorder you will not recognize failure either. It's just that leaders who feed disorder, need disorder. So you cannot justify disorder and then complain over lack.

And why would any leader ever need disorder? *Chaos is how he/she controls their environment and their people.* People who feed disorder are not juiced at forward progress as much as they are juiced by the rush of digging themselves out from another hole. People who feed disorder are really feeding their significance amongst inferior and incompetent people.

It's like this: *incompetence is the result of demanding something bigger out of your life without first demanding something bigger out of your standard of leadership to get it.*

CEO FACT:

You will not master success, either professional or personal. You will only master what causes success.

Success is as much of a systematic process as is failure. Systematic meaning, an order or regiment of values that we are willing to repeat over and over again.

So, you will master managing your money right long before you will master being financially independent.

You will master developing an uncommon work ethic long before it is your name on the front of the company.

You will master eating right long before you will master being in better shape.

Making personal progress is not just an issue of winning the battle of self-discipline either. That alone is depressing, seeing how we can regiment ourselves right out of having any fun in life whatsoever. But it is about becoming better at what will produce the right results for our life than we are at producing the wrong ones.

Success is never inherited. Money is inherited, and success is not money. Success is created by habitual routine, restructured game plan, and decisive values.

So, for people, say like college coaching legend, John Wooden, or talk show icon, Oprah Winfrey, success simply came from the right things they were willing to refine and then keep repeating over and over again.

The issue of mediocrity is not a discipline issue either; *it is a vision issue.* Meaning, we can only refine our systems for success at the level that our personal vision has either agreed to or refused to live without the level of success we are supposed to have.

No, this does not mean that everything we want now, we get now. But is does mean that life does not come down to some people who are just naturally more decisive versus some who are not. It comes down to some people who have less time to live without prosperity in an area versus some people who apparently have more.

1.

Procedurize anything that you want to succeed in more than once.

No, I don't mean carry around a five inch thick manual just for knowing how to do the laundry or take the kids to the park. But success only responds to routine, not luck.

The desire to not have chaos will not remove chaos like the detailed plan of how not to have any will.

So, you and I cannot succeed beyond how much our current system is built to accommodate success. Meaning, a system for achieving your goals, maintaining order, et cetera.

To say that structure limits you would be a gross error heralded only by the lazy. Structure does not limit you. It removes stress. Stress limits you. So, anything productive that you cannot do more than once is just luck.

What is a procedure? A procedure is the written and established guideline for how you want a specific area of your vision to function. A procedure is also so that you can use your mind for creativity more than for memory. Meaning, everything you have to remember to do because of a lack of order will just hinder everything you could be creative to do if the right system freed you to do it.

Why do you need a procedure? Anything verbal can be debated. Anything written can only be followed.

Even as a leader of others, you cannot even tell who will produce the right or wrong results under your leadership until you see how much they will either follow a procedure or ignore one. Those who will not believe in your procedures will not believe in your goal either.

Besides, you cannot assume that those serving you will give you more than what your training and procedures told them you needed.

How do you write a procedure? Think of every possible problem you could ever have in every possible area of achieving your goals and then write a solution for how you can both solve such a problem and avoid them from repeating themselves.

But what if I cannot anticipate every kind of problem I could encounter? Sooner or later you will.

Problems expose loopholes. Loopholes are where destructive patterns and destructive people hide out.

It is never isolated problems that sink a leader, only ongoing problems that do.

2.

Work harder to create something good than you do to get rid of something bad.

Wrong habits and wrong people do not just leave. Right habits and right people replace them.

So, you will never change something bad. You will only create something good and the entry of what is right will force the exit of what is not.

One reason is because the only things that ever stop us are never in front of us. *They are inside of us.*

So, in the long run people really do not have enemies. They have dysfunctional parts of themselves that are no bigger than who their enemies are that their enemies use as leverage against them. And while you may consider your enemies to be betrayal, letdowns beyond your control, abusive people, et cetera, except for extreme physical or mental handicap, nothing can be an enemy unless it is allowed to work with something defective inside of you to shut you down.

3.

Where are you participating with abusive or mediocre relationships as your way of covering for your own low standard?

Mediocre relationships cannot help you sustain greatness . . . they can only drain it.

So, sabotage will only take place through people who have connected with your weaknesses more than your integrity. Abusive relationships are simply when we connect with people without a greater standard and then punish them for not being able to produce a greater result.

Where is your behavior or personal integrity off course with where you need to be in this area?

How would the person you want to be handle this area differently?

Leadership is never just about managing a situation. It is about managing who you are in a situation.

12

INCREASE WILL ONLY RESPOND TO ANYTHING THAT IS MANAGED.

All success in life comes down to five issues: *protecting your time, managing your money, feeding your relationships, owning your vision, and protecting your body.*

This is because none of us were given success. We were given time, resources, connections, ideas, and a physical temple to facilitate success with. How we manage these elements determines how much we manage our success.

And this is the issue. Your success will never be the result of doing something good occasionally, and consistency will never be the result of only doing things that are difficult.

So where you are managing inconsistency you are managing lack. Consistency is such a phenomenal force in that excellence as we discussed in the previous chapter, cannot even be considered excellence unless consistency is fueling it. In other words, *excellence without consistency is not excellence. It is mediocrity with isolated splashes of brilliance interwoven throughout it.*

One reason for inconsistency will be gaps in your focus. Another reason will be gaps in your character.

Gaps in your focus determine what you are distracted by. Gaps in your character determine how long you stay distracted.

For this reason, all success in anything comes down to the right things you are willing to do habitually more than occasionally. This is why champions only want to be remembered for what they finish.

Whereas as losers assume they should be remembered for just making an effort.

CEO FACT:

You will stop doing right things consistently long before you will lose everything right that you have.

Successful people are only made by successful regiments. Which is why *nothing will alter your life until it alters your daily routine.*

It's like this: Life is a collection of days. What we do in a day will determine what we become in a lifetime.

This is why no person arrives at success because of one good day, nor do they arrive at failure because of one bad day. So, while our life will be motivated by a dream, it is made by a routine. Meaning you cannot own your dreams and goals until you can effectively own twenty-four hours.

There is no such thing as credibility without consistency. So, the wrong parts of you will only balk at the right things that you do consistently.

"But Konrad, I'm more of a spontaneous person."

You mean a moody achiever. Yes, I adamantly believe in the power of spontaneity. Anything creatively profound has bursts to it. But the problem with moods is they rob consistency, and inconsistency is the only leverage we give to our weaknesses.

So, the most productive people wake up, go to bed, work, and eat dinner at least through the week at the same time every day. *It's called a regiment.*

Maybe one out of a hundred days goes right on its own. The other ninety-nine we make go right because of what we force to comply with our priorities of a day. So you will only have a problem with managing a successful regiment when you have a problem managing excuses or codependence.

And personally, as a leader and employer of people, one way that I can tell when someone has checked out on where they are is by observing the things they stop doing. Meaning, everything we stop doing consistently simply reveals where we no longer want to be.

Whether a marriage, a slim waistline, or a fine-tuned office, people stop doing right things to be where they are sometimes several months before they physically leave. Same thing happens on a personal level. *We stop doing successful things over time just before any success that we have leaves us.*

CEO FACT:

You will never finish any goal that is huge, if you are not willing to learn the art of managing momentum.

Managing momentum requires four key elements to start.

First, managing a big goal in achievable stages. Meaning, realistic stages.

We do not reach breakthrough levels of success in any area until the momentum of our progress is as big as the presence of our confidence and the accuracy of our wisdom.

That is what momentum is. It is the connection of several smaller steps together to produce a fluid movement of achievement. So if your goals are not defined in believable stages, then they will become easily resented. Without momentum you only end up doubting and second guessing what you could accomplish.

Secondly, managing momentum demands that you do at least one right thing every day that is taking you towards your most important goals.

Let's review again. Only one in a hundred days goes how you want it to. The other ninety-nine you will have to demand that some part of them goes how you need them to based on the things you refuse to accept defeat in.

Thirdly, managing momentum will require you to pace your day to have at least one escape for you.

Escapes retool the mind. If you have no time to clear your mind, you will have no time to refine your plan.

Remember: *mental toughness beats passive skill any day.* So failure will never take place because your goal told you it could not be achieved, but because your tired mind did, and the rest of your behavior and decisions followed.

Lastly, managing momentum will require you to schedule your desired progress.

The great cosmetic entrepreneur, Mary Kay Ash, would outline her seven biggest priorities to do for the next day. It's where you do not plan daily progress that you will only feel daily hostility. Progress is oxygen; whereas frustration is suffocating.

CEO FACT:

Until you can recognize the character or lack of it in your habits, structure, and relationships you will be unable to recognize the pace to either your success or your breakdown.

Part of removing a personal or professional limitation is changing either the habit, the system, or the relationship that is making that limitation too easy to exist.

This is what burnout is. *Burnout is simply the result of allowing the wrong things to drain the right things out of you.* Burnout is only facilitated by our attempts to live life on a level that we are not making enough strategic growth changes to support.

It's like this. Some of us only sustain the things that are in our heart to obtain, good or bad. Meaning, whatever we have time for, we get. So, how you spend your time says everything about the priorities you have. It is our priorities that expose our true values good or bad.

For example, a married person says to me they want to make their marriage work. I just watch what they spend their time in. What we spend our time in determines what we really want.

This is why many people battle so badly with lying to themselves. They say they want things that they put no real time into getting past a momentary compulsive burst or the motivational speeches that push them.

Why? They are afraid to acknowledge that they really do not want in their heart commitment what they say they do in their soulish emotion. So you can sell the lie as long as you do not tell anyone else what you say you want that a lack of time spent to get it will expose differently.

Don't believe me? I've watched people with children get offered last minute concert tickets. It is actually humorous to watch how far they will stretch the limits of a babysitter that they normally would not consider just to accommodate such a rare night out. Because after all, *"The Rolling Stones just don't tour that often."*

Try the rare markdown at Neiman Marcus or the long holiday weekend. Any of us can move heaven and earth for what we really want. Self-improvement in anything is no different.

Then there is *"expediential people,"* as Tony Robbins would call them, who are people that do not spend their time on pettiness or drama.

They will not take five days to do what they could have done in one. They refuse to place million-dollar energy into $2.99 issues.

So, a couple on the split will drag out a divorce or a setback until they have produced way more damage then needed simply because that is all they had time for.

This is the reality. The greatest proof of a lack of successful priorities is exposed in the chaos you have time for and the drama you manage.

So where you have time to be sloppy then you will manage disorder. But if you only have time to move forward, then you will manage prosperity.

CEO FACT:

Anything great that you want that cannot currently enter your life just means there is no room for it to be there.

We only manage what we make room for. We make room for what we want.

Want a better marriage? Make room for it.

Want healthier friends? Make room for them.

Want more money? Make room for it.

Want a healthier body? Make room for it.

Want a more fulfilling lifestyle? Make room for it.

If what you have is not what you are supposed to have, then stop making room for it to be there.

How? Stop using your paradigms, behavior, habits, decisions, diets, excuses, and associations to accommodate its existence. Got it now?

CEO FACT:

What you will not put into your body, your body will not put into your dreams.

Prosperity does not respond to potential. It only responds to what is managed properly. Your body is no different.

It is your body that is the vehicle for your dreams. So when you rob your body, you are giving your limitations permission to rob your dreams.

And when it comes to physical health, it is not merely about loving your body. It is more about loving your potential. It is only where we are demanding more out of our bodies than what we are putting into it, that we are really managing burnout instead. Since after all, people who only love their bodies are really just resenting their insecurity.

Tired eyes cannot see fresh opportunity. Meaning, exhaustion is the last stage before elimination.

President Eisenhower would not make any important decisions after 3:00 PM because of how much he knew that he would not be as mentally sharp.

It is okay to be consumed with your goal as long as you know where your recovery points are to your goal.

This is why great leaders achieve more—because they know how to protect their downtime as much as they do their creativity.

So exhaustion is what allows your enemies to take what they could have never taken had you been alert.

And exhaustion can be just as much the result of being too ineffective as it can be being too productive. Meaning, some people are exhausted from managing their lives going nowhere.

Which is why willful physical deterioration is not about a person void of motivation, but rather about a person void of a dream.

So, when it comes to taking care of the physical you, you will only damage what you have no vision to use productively later down the road.

For example, people who smoke say things like *"smoking relaxes me."* But you cannot have anything in your life whether cigarettes or credit cards that pleasures you now, but destroys you later.

The misconception? *People who live healthy must love the sacrifice.* Not really. They just love the end result.

Remember this: *Super-achieving is not about living without rest. It is about living without disorder.*

1.

Manage your time.

Managing your time is not about being good at multitasking. It is about not being good at being lost.

People who manage their time well know what time it is. Meaning, they know when it is time to push, prepare, restructure and when it is time to play.

Time is never the ally of those who talk but don't move. Time only works for movers and shakers.

Time is the only chance you have at not having to constantly manage the damage of assumption. This is because time never lies about what it reveals.

It reveals direction, it reveals motive. It tells us how far and how deep we can or cannot go with anything or anyone.

Time is also the only element that brings the parts of our decisions together that we could not control to come together without the element of proper timing.

Time is also your greatest weapon against costly decisions because time can only bring realistic perspectives to the table and not emotional ones.

And protecting your time is not about being rude or non-relational. It is about not being afraid to resent an unproductive pace. Meaning people who are rude are only protecting ego, *not time.*

2.

See a nutritionist and a personal trainer.

You must be as careful about what you put into your body as you are the people you let tell you to do it.

This means not going to the local generic vitamin store in the mall where the guy with no neck or the soccer mom who needed a part-time job or the sixteen-year-old who thinks that X-Box should be an Olympic event, tells you that everything should work for you. This also means not just buying vitamins at random because the labels looked promising.

Go to a trained doctor who can analyze your diet, your metabolism, et cetera, and not just sell you ginseng because it will pick you up. *Clarity is about how you feel about yourself and not about how some ginkgo pill can solve your memory problems.*

A proper diet is about knowing good fat from bad fat. It is about knowing what times in the day to eat to maintain energy. Remember: *people live with bad esteem before they live with bad nutritional habits.*

3.

Exercise.

None of us ever improve what we do not believe in.

Capable people who do not exercise are having personal vision problems, not physical ones.

So, consult a personal trainer who can coach you more about form, breathing, and stress rather than bulk. Anyone can make you look like the poster child for steroids, but not everyone can help you burn fat and build strength.

Where is your behavior or personal integrity off course with where you need to be in this area?

How would the person you want to be handle this area differently?

REALITY CHECK

Leadership is never about being good at managing resources. Rather, it is an issue of being good at managing your end result and then making resources conform.

13

MANAGING YOUR MONEY WILL BE THE ONLY DIFFERENCE BETWEEN PLANNING AND MOVEMENT.

You cannot enjoy making money and not enjoy managing it. Without money, all we end up talking about is everything we could do if we just had some.

So, to assume that you can protect your dreams and goals and not protect the money needed to facilitate them is only delusional.

CEO FACT:

Everyone else in your life will enjoy spending your money and taking your money, but you will have to enjoy managing it.

Managing your money is the only chance you have at multiplying it. So if you cannot make a hundred dollars go right, then having a thousand will only accelerate your self-destruction.

Managing your personal money comes down to managing your piles of it. *(Nice picture isn't it?)*

Suze Orman is a much better teacher on this than I, but some good piles to start with are *bills, savings, and fun.*

And the secret is not to wait for one pile to be taken care of before you feed the other piles.

1. Bills. There is not a lot to say about bills other than we have them. Ideally most financial advisers recommend tailoring your monthly overhead to 70 percent of your net monthly income.

Streamlining things through automatic deposit and withdrawal as well as online accounting can minimize stress.

2. A storehouse. Anyone can make plans to manage pressure. Only smart people make plans to live above as much of it as possible.

Take the amount of what your weekly overhead is and then begin saving towards as many of those weeks in the bank as you can.

3. Fun money. This is the comfort dinners, comfort concert tickets, and the comfort mocha lattes at your favorite coffee place.

Don't fall for the myth that *"as soon as I can pay off debt, then I will have more to place in my fun pile."* All discipline has to see at least some reward or else we end up with too much resentment to stay disciplined.

CEO FACT:

If you want to leave debt, then hate debt.

Debt is the allusion that makes us appear richer than we actually are. Debt is also a dictator. Where you live with what is tight, you will also live with what is handicapped.

And yes, there is obviously good debt and bad debt. And no, not all debt is avoidable. But the type of bad debt from excessive credit or borrowing that is created by a weakness to medicate a weakness is.

The problem with most people in too much debt is not the debt. It is actually the perverted mentality that says, *"my value is enhanced because so many places want to give me credit."* That is not a sign of personal value. It is only a sign of personal destruction.

Remember: *impatience will eventually place you in situations that miracles will be forced to bail you out of.*

- *See a financial planner if need be, face to face in your area who has a reputable track record for debt consolidation.* Get references for other local people in your area whom he/she has helped.
- *A credit repair person is also very good.*

➤ *Then build your personal portfolio of what you pay cash to own.*

"Yes, but it was no payments or interest until the year the apocalypse would take place." Doesn't matter. You will only enjoy what you do not owe.

1.

Sign your own checks.

Everyone else in your life will enjoy spending your money. You will have to enjoy managing how much they spend.

Some of the richest people in the world still sign their own checks because of one reason. *Uncommon leaders do not live with their pulse on who is managing their money. They live with their pulse on their money.*

2.

Live off of the top rather than off of the bottom.

Corporate leaders and governments do this more frequently than the average nine to fiver, but it can work for anyone.

Make a long-term goal of placing one or several years of your operating budget in a capitol reserve and then spend for your projects, expansion, and your overhead above that.

3.

Don't be afraid when you can, to use your money to remove the limits to your time.

This is not an issue about not saving when you can. Even the average rich person loves to save. But uncommon leaders only succeed to the level of what consumes their time. And often the dilemma of expanding our responsibilities is an issue of vision before it is an issue of resources.

For example, smart millionaires and billionaires do not have cooks, chauffeurs, caretakers, personal valets, or even personal pilots because they want the world to know they are rich. Most, have them because of what these various people give them in return, *the gift of time.*

It's one thing if mowing your own grass or running your own errands is an escape for you. It's another if it is a detour.

Personally, I don't pay someone else to mow my grass or clean my pool because I am so wealthy and that kind of dirty work is beneath me. My vision and even the downtime from my vision happens to be worth more than grass and pool scum. So my vision is worth a few extra bucks that I spend on protecting my focus.

4.

Always use the weapon of giving.

Your goals are never the proof that you believe in your future. Your seed is. This is the other element of managing money; *the part about giving it.*

The first law ever instituted into the earth was the law of seedtime and harvest. Meaning what you sow, you will reap. So a seed goes into the earth and a harvest comes from it. A seed goes into a womb, and a life is conceived.

It's like this: *You cannot manage what you cannot multiply.* Giving is a law. Not a personality trait or a religion.

This is why it takes a visionary to be a giver, and it takes a giver to be a visionary. In other words, what we have, that we are willing to sow for what we want that we would never have, if we were to just hold onto it in the hopes of it getting bigger.

Anyone can dream. Not everyone can see the potential of something they have in their hand enough to release it as the seed that can create that dream. So, it is only where our giving stops that our movement stops with it.

This is because of what a seed is. It is something that we either have because of our position, our resources, or our pocketbook that can be used as a weapon for movement instead of just an issue of self-gratification.

No, this is not about giving everything you have out of some vow of poverty. None of us can help anyone through poverty. But it is about the reality of giving that *the moment we want to leave today we will have to leave something in today.* Meaning, *when you keep what you have, you will stay where you are.*

True prosperity can only respond to purpose. So, giving is not about mastering generosity but rather about mastering vision. God will never prosper you to make you stand out to people more than to be the solution for them.

Where is your behavior or personal integrity off course with where you need to be in this area?

How would the person you want to be handle this area differently?

Leadership is always revealed through approach. Approach is always the proof of the type of leader you are either not afraid to be or are okay not to be as long as those you are leading never know the difference.

14

WHATEVER IS NOT ALLOWED TO BEAT YOU IN YOUR MIND, WILL NOT BE ALLOWED TO BEAT YOU ON YOUR BATTLEFIELD EITHER.

Personal defeat is never the result of a limited arsenal more than a limited mind. Which is why every rut you will ever be stuck in will have the parts of a weak mind holding you hostage.

One reason is because most things that have the power to defeat us never defeat us because of how big they are but because of how we choose to view them.

This has nothing to do with whether we have a legitimate right to feel pain or injustice in something. But, *how we handle ourselves is determined by how we see ourselves in any situation.*

Personally, I was orphaned a great deal growing up.

So as an adult, anytime I would experience betrayal or abandonment from someone closest to me, my first response would be to accept the pain from an orphaned position. My repeated unhealthy and very powerless approaches in these situations were based on how I saw myself based on what I had always known. So we can only use dysfunctional and perverted coping skills to compensate for where we lack a healthy grasp of any situation and who we are in that situation.

No, this is not to say that we can use our minds to pretend that the undesirable parts of reality that exist for us, in some alternative fantasy reality, really don't. But there will never be one conflict in our lives big or small that we cannot change our position in by changing our perspective of it first. There will never be one mountain so big that we cannot conquer without changing what we see about the mountain.

Which means narrow-mindedness, which is what passive people describe instead as *"just being cautious,"* does not really help you remain cautious either. It only helps you remain stuck while you use denial to explain your loss.

CEO FACT:

There will always be a bigger perspective of any problem that can move you past a problem that is usually never on the surface of the problem. Your only problem will be refusing to let go of the pain of the problem long enough to go beyond the surface and grab it.

One normal day in late 2003 the shocking news on my television told of three beautiful sisters all under seventeen who were on their way to the wedding practice of their older brother in rural Minnesota.

A drunk driver hit them and killed all three sisters. The small town was in deep mourning. But when the newscaster interviewed the mother, who was being strong despite of deep grieving, all that she said was, *"They went to a better wedding today in heaven."*

No one would have faulted her if she was even so grief stricken that she could not talk to the media much less make it through the funeral. But this mother took her pain and made it bow to a perspective of such a horrible incident that prevented her from sinking deeper in her pain, much less even using it as the platform for her own self-destruction.

There is nothing painful, destructive, or desperate that we cannot exit without a change in how we view it. And no conflict dominates us unless a part of it is bigger than our current attitude and maturity level.

So often times, we cannot imagine a perspective greater than our pain or frustration only because we are waiting for feelings to change before our thinking does.

And where do these perspective changes come from?

All broadening of our perspective must do battle with wounded and, at times, selfish feelings before anything is different. Wounded feelings are where we have a right to feel injustice. But wounded feelings become selfish feelings the moment we build the core of our behavior around being wounded.

It is not the reality of any problem that we medicate anyhow. We only medicate what we are embracing about what a narrow perspective is telling us about the problem. *The injustice, however, of a problem is only one part of any problem. The solution is never in the injustice. The solution is in the approach. Healthy approaches are only contained inside of a healed perspective.*

So, where you are not sure that you want to see a bigger picture of any situation, you are probably not sure of the kinds of personal changes you would be willing to make in order to resolve the situation.

CEO FACT:

Our mind only keeps going through doors of anxiety or self-destruction when it has no doors of truth to go through instead.

You will never stop caving at the same things until you are willing to change what you believe about them and why.

To do this you will first have to let yourself be challenged by bigger thinkers. Then you will have to stop negotiating with fear. Fear is an allusion, whereas truth is reality.

Fear can only intimidate you by using reason to do it. Meaning reason is what makes fear make sense. And fear will only make sense to the helpless parts of you.

For example, people do not always participate with insanity or abuse because they like it, but because fear convinces them they have no other choice.

This is why all fear usually exploits one thing: *what we may likely lose if we were to stop handling things by fear.* Pain makes everything narrow. It shrinks perspective because it suffocates. And there is only one thing that breeds from narrow pain: *passivity.*

For example, people do not live in miserable situations for several years. They live in a passive approach because of a narrow perspective to self-esteem for several years.

Meaning, people only stay stuck in what they have no healthy view of themselves to pull themselves through. So their narrow view, which is also their wounded view, is linked to their absence of self-respect in that area. Since we only participate with anything abusive because of how we see ourselves and not how we see the abusers.

So being stuck in anything only means that a problem exists. It does not mean that answers don't.

CEO FACT:

We can only solve any problem to the degree that we can solve our perspective of the problem first.

Just before every new level of success in your life will be the challenge to decrease what you consider to be overwhelming. Meaning, the challenge is to shrink your definition of what you have considered to be impossible up until that point. This is also the time when we battle with the issues within us that were at one time real, but have now been allowed to be exaggerated for the purpose of staying self-protected.

Attorneys will do this. They will take a level three issue and inflate it to a level seven issue just to get the extra mileage from the inflated controversy of it to add to their case. Crooked cops will do this with evidence.

The press will do this with hearsay versus truth; *exaggerate something as a means of using it for what they need it to be, in order to cover for everything they fear it is not.*

Guess what. We do this also, where we are revolting against our greatest personal growth by reciting certain hurts, insecurities, and letdowns in a light of being more impossible to get over or forgive then what they really are.

In other words, we need something that happened years ago to still be as big of a deal as if it just happened last night. *None of us can move on from anything painful or unjust until we are willing to move on from the people we were in those situations.*

This is one reason why people can spend years in therapy for personal pain. They are not too different now from the people they were in the situations they were so hurt by. Yesterday's pain is only permitted to hold the same credibility with us today when we are the ones not really different. People who are different now, move on. Not because their pain was not real, but rather because they are not the same people that yesterday hurt anymore.

This is never because of the seriousness of the crime, more than where the crime has just exposed where we failed to grow as individuals in the time since then. So, who exploited our lack of personal growth is blamed more than where we were not growing is.

People will do this where they do not want to work through relational issues. They will constantly keep yesterday's disappointments fresh in order to keep their anger fueled enough to justify not having to reconcile, forgive, et cetera. So, past circumstances and relationships are blamed for the guilt we feel from our own lack of personal improvements.

This is also where many people live immobilized by severe depression, uncontrollable grieving, meltdowns, nervous breakdowns, et cetera, when there is no distinctive line between their yesterday and today. It is all one big cluttered hodgepodge of good overlapping with bad, outdated overlapping with relevant. This is because there has been no distinctive personal growth that has placed more and more distance between the way things were versus the way they can be now.

The reason for this lack of growth is the dominance of a wounded perspective, which is also a selfish perspective. Which also is silencing any capacity to make healthy decisions that can only be made through an honest perspective.

The secret to growth in anything is always in the realm of what is bigger than what we felt.

Yes, certain aspects of yesterday's pain was for all of us as large as life while we were in the midst of encountering it. Abuse, abandonment, betrayal, divorce, bankruptcy, infidelity, failure, et cetera. However, *yesterday was only supposed to be real yesterday.* So, where we have still never matured our way out of yesterday, then yesterday is no longer a reality; *it's an exaggeration.*

Meaning, it's an exaggeration of where we are now forced to keep reusing the severity of past things in order to keep the severity level as real today as it was yesterday.

This is in order to justify our own lazy character as well as destructive behavior.

This is one reason why forgiveness is so misunderstood. It is impossible to forgive where you have been hurt when you are still in many ways the same person you were when you were hurt.

It is impossible to forgive from feelings. We're just not built to do that. Forgiveness is only possible from a position of personal progress. Meaning, we do not need the pain to become distant in order for us to make better changes.

CEO FACT:

The kind of thoughts that you allow your mind to continually be seeded with will be a clue to the kinds of success or failure you are headed for.

Timothy McVeigh acknowledged that he thought about getting even with the FBI for over one year before he carried out a terrorist act of blowing up the Federal Building in Oklahoma City killing 168 innocent people in 1996.

Thoughts are a prelude to becoming. So people just do not commit suicide. They think about hopelessness until death becomes a logical answer. People can meditate on suicide or success just before they achieve it.

This is because *no thought is ever just a thought. It is the beginning of what has several dimensions of deeper impact whether good or bad.*

No, you do not have to give into destructive thoughts. But you do have to flush negative thoughts through more functional filters than just dismissing them as coincidental, minimal or accept them because they are familiar.

To fix this it will require work to continually change how long your focus can stay broken. Meaning, part of strengthening healthy focus lies in how fast you can adjust it. Boxers have sixty seconds in between rounds. Football players have one half-time. *Iron focus is not about skill; it is about adjustments and how fast you decide to make them.*

1.

Condition your mind to finish.

Champions just don't finish; they think like finishers.

Finishers are not just people with a vision for greatness. They are people who will go to the other side of anything inconvenient or handicapped to get it.

➤ *What can't you leave earth without fulfilling?*

➤ *What can't you live another year without experiencing significant change in?*

Finishers think in terms of what is nonnegotiable not to attain. They also do not meditate on anything that can take them backwards for very long.

And it's not that finishers have such an anxiety free mind, it's just that they have a more guarded one.

2.

Where is your mind not breaking the ceiling?

Our church entered a building program, which as history has it more churches fall apart during times of expansion than actually make it through it. But the one thing that I always kept in front of our church during this process was the truth that *small size churches are not what fail during building programs, small-minded churches do.*

Wealth, degrees, friends, influence, . . . nothing will ever be as big of a resource to your future as what is between your ears. So you have to ask yourself, *where are you still uncomfortable with breaking through in something?*

Until you become comfortable with fulfillment on another level, you will never stop seeing the things that are overwhelming to you any differently.

For me personally, my fiancée at the time, and I gave a large sum of money to a national organization. The amount staggered me mentally, but I knew we were supposed to do it.

It also happened to be four weeks before our wedding that we did this. So, there went our honeymoon savings.

But while I kept waiting to see the obvious results back to us in doing such a charitable thing, I had missed the biggest thing that it did; *it changed the way I looked at that level of finances and that level of risk taking.*

I began functioning on a whole new mental level not because I became inherently wealthy, but because I never again saw the level I was on as being the big deal I was treating it as.

Sure we can argue, *"What if that is all you have ever known or you come from poverty?"* Of course, I was guilty of both of these. But at some point we have to decide that we are going to take steps for purpose sake that have nothing to do with background.

➤ *Where do you keep backing down?* You will always know where you are not breaking your mental ceiling about something because you keep backing down for the same reasons. Anyplace where we keep backing down instead of breaking through, we just end up shifting around the same problems or the same lack, instead of stretching past it.

3

Adapt this principle as a filter for processing disappointment: everything begins NOW! Yesterday is over. What has to be different now is not dependent on what it was before.

Where is your behavior or personal integrity off course with where you need to be in this area?

____

____

____

____

____

____

____

How would the person you want to be handle this area differently?

____

____

____

____

____

____

____

Leadership is never developed through the presence of obstacles more than what you refuse to allow an obstacle to become.

15

YOU WILL ALWAYS BECOME COMFORTABLE WITH WHAT CAN DERAIL YOU JUST BEFORE IT DOES.

This was Samson's problem with Delilah. *He became comfortable with her before he became destroyed by her.*

She made Samson comfortable before she made him powerless. She stroked his hair before she cut it off.

She developed appeal with him just before she stripped him of his power.

This is the only way that destruction works; *you become comfortable with destruction before you become derailed by it.*

With Delilah this was not a gender issue, but rather a self-destruction issue. In that *anything that can destroy you will first be permitted to develop appeal with you before it does.* Meaning, Delilah could not force Samson to reveal his secrets of power, but she could make him comfortable with danger.

The executives at Enron became comfortable with price gauging. Of course, now some of them are uncomfortable with jail.

Married couples get comfortable with strife. Of course, then they become uncomfortable with divorce attorneys and custody settlements. *Comfort on a vacation is necessary. But comfort with rage, depression, greed, or broken focus is downright dangerous.*

CEO FACT:

You cannot befriend what can derail you and then hate it after it does.

Our greatest self-destruction only takes place where we are reasoning with our greatest passivity.

So, the only type of weaknesses you will never overcome will be the weaknesses that you still enjoy participating in.

In others words, *leaders may fail once because of a lack of insight. But they will fail twice because of a lack of concern.*

So, whatever type of destructiveness that you permit around you the first time can be because of what is lacking in someone else. But when you permit it the second time it will be the result of what is lacking in you.

And while many of us may have *learned* abuse as children, we only *tolerate* abuse as adults. Meaning, as children we accepted what we had no choice over.

But as adults we only tolerate what fear and our lack of self-respect tells us we have no choice not to. And anything that we can tolerate we cannot change.

CEO FACT:

You will never think beyond your backbone.

Leaders never think deeper than their foundation.

Leaders never think healthier than their foundation.

It is where we lack depth in specific areas as leaders that reflects in the inappropriate ways that we handle things.

The problem is that most people have stubbornness and then call it backbone. Stubbornness however, is not backbone. Backbone is the result of values that are nonnegotiable that are the result of loving truth enough to embrace order, while loving yourself enough to enforce it. Stubbornness on the other hand, is self-protection. It is worshiping your own version of reality too much past the point of accountability to be correct more than unique. Which is also why none of us can determine our backbone until we can determine what we will not keep doing the same wrong way. It is at this point where we are wrestling with backbone that we are really still deciding what we are not so sure we are ready to take ownership of the success of.

This is also one reason why the stereotypical motivational seminar "be a big thinker" is not always accurate.

You can dream as big as you want. But your dreams will have to experience a character change before they will experience a mentality change in order to achieve them. So you will have to become the person that can achieve your dreams before you will achieve them.

Meaning, what you keep doing wrong that is the result of what you keep being wrong.

And since we only wrestle with backbone where we do not wrestle against fear or pride enough, none of us ever stay stuck in anything we resent being stuck in. We actually have a mentality to be stuck there. Meaning, people don't just have hang-ups. They have a belief system that babysits hang-ups.

They have not decided how different they really want their life to be in certain defective areas.

For example, have you ever asked yourself, *"Where is my emotional age not as high as my physical age?"*

Don't think it is a relevant question? It most certainly is, when you are forty on your driver's license, but fifteen in your coping skills. Our emotional age stops wherever our backbone does for growth .

How can you tell? None of us can ever live on a level that our values cannot enforce. This is the issue: wherever our backbone stops, we will just construct a belief system within ourselves that enables us to justify living without something better that God was trying to give us.

CEO FACT:

Your real enemies will never emerge until your real purpose poses a threat.

Anything that can derail you will have to use something in you to do it. Here are a few clues.

Deception will be an enemy because you are only ripe for sabotage in the areas where you lack enough truth. So, adversity never beats you until your own distortions of truth beat you first.

Fear will be an enemy the moment the strategy for where you are going is not bigger than the memories of where you came from and the excuses of why you have not gone any further.

Hopelessness will be an enemy the moment you equate having no answers with having no purpose. Hopelessness is only as permanent as a limited perspective and a powerless approach.

Rejection will be an enemy the moment you cannot move beyond the people who do not see you through the eyes of what you believe they should.

Some days rejection can also be God's way of sparing you from who you would later regret had they actually accepted you.

Vulnerability will be an enemy because your enemy fears anything expired or unproductive that you are willing to walk away from.

Nothing unnecessary will ever immobilize you until it is permitted to obligate you to what is not your responsibility to fix or tolerate.

Criticism will be an enemy the moment you cannot recover from the opinions of others who see little need for your method or your message.

Remember: You will never be falsely judged by someone who is more complete than you. So, you will have to know the difference between honest evaluation and irrelevant attack, or you will leave yourself no latitude to benefit from the insight of disagreement.

CEO FACT:

Whatever has your attention will have your direction.

Every failure in your life will be traced to a failure in your focus first.

Hitler saw a Europe that could be extinguished of an entire Jewish culture. Terrorist saw planes crashing into high-rise buildings in New York City and Washington D.C. on 9/11. *Leaders see things before they reach for them, good or bad.* Without understanding the lure of destructive traps, you will end up sounding more magical than realistic about your derailments.

Meaning, you will say things like, "*. . . and one day I just found myself in an affair, hooked on some bad habit, et cetera. Or one day I just ended up broke.*" The truth be told, you and I can only end up at where we are looking first.

This is because focus is not a gift. It is a force. So before King David ever committed adultery with another man's wife, named Bathsheba, only to impregnate her and have her husband killed to cover it up, he could not stop looking at her (see 2 Samuel 11).

Before David Yongi Cho ever built the largest church in the world in Seoul, South Korea, he would spend hours every day looking at the masses of Korean people out from his leased office space atop a building overlooking downtown Seoul.

People spend weeks, months, and sometimes years seeing themselves becoming hooked to a dangerous addiction or becoming engaged in an extramarital affair.

Many criminals do the same thing before they even commit their first crime. *Plans are birthed by photographs, good or bad.*

So the reality is *wherever you do not want to end up you cannot spend any time looking at everything that could take you there.*

For example, people just don't end up in divorce court. They just don't end up a hundred pounds overweight. They just don't end up with unfulfilled lifestyles. They look at the kinds of lazy, hurt, and self-centered perspectives that can take them there, and that is what steers their habits, relationships, and decisions in that direction.

CEO FACT:

Anything that can cause derailment has to enter our sights before it enters our life.

All of us are led by what voids, needs, or desires captivate our sight the most. So, where unhealthy patterns are concerned, we can only stop repeating what we are willing to wrestle enough with our own selfish feelings to see differently.

Place the color pink in front of a body builder and they lose over one third of their strength. Place red in front of a person, and they become aggressive. A black suit at a meeting is more intimidating than a blue one.

A gray suit says that you can be more neutral.

Place beige in front of an employee and they become lethargic. Some believe taupe is soothing.

Watch a hamburger commercial at nine at night and you are immediately debating over getting up to go get one.

The reality is that everything we look at has an effect on us. *Whatever we look at the longest determines what we will go the farthest to obtain, good or bad.*

Keep looking at a past mistake.

Keep looking at an infidelity you were a victim of.

Keep looking at a painful loss you still have no answers for. We do not just go off course. We do not just lose valuable things to us. We become captivated with what takes us off course and with what can facilitate loss.

Your direction in life will be molded around anything you cannot take your eyes off of. Which is why everything you look at will either have the power to drain you or sustain you. Pull you through, or pull you under. So we do not magically become healthy in our lives. We become captivated with what being healthy is.

CEO FACT:

You are only ever one focus change away from a desired goal.

Distractions have to require your permission before they can cause your derailment.

None of us have varying levels of focus. We only have varying levels of insight on how to use it and varying levels of integrity on how to protect it. This is one area where God leveled the playing field for everyone.

However, destructive focus is only the result of lazy focus. Meaning distorted focus is passive focus.

Passive focus is simply the result of where we refuse to deal with distractions. Which means no distraction ever starts as big as it can become until our passivity to deal with it gives it size.

An eighty-plus-year-old mentor once told it to me this way: *never breathe life into anything that does not need to live.* Meaning, most distractions are only distractions because we say that they are. It is how we deal with the average distraction that gives it size and life.

So, many people will give a level two distraction level eight attention simply because they have nothing else better in their lives to exert creative energy on. Refereeing conflict is safer for them than taking risks on positive change.

Which is also one reason why we can get re-focused as fast as we can get distracted. Getting re-focused in anything will never be as hard as getting past our own hurt feelings and our own distorted perspectives will.

1.

Stop assuming that other people will want to protect your focus.

Success is the result of guarding your focus. Failure is just the result of assuming others would.

Protecting your focus does not mean being rude. Rude people only protect ego, not productivity.

Other people protect what is big to them, not what is big to you. So, protecting your focus means protecting the most productive habits, routine, and environment that determines the most productive you.

Any productive focus will only offend those not permitted to distract it. It's just that those who do not mind distracting you will not mind watching you fail either.

➤ *You will only defend what is incompetent or inappropriate until failure strips you of an argument.* It's just that when you crash, dysfunction or perversion is not going to defend you. So, do not defend them while you are still standing.

Dysfunction never makes us look good. As a matter of fact it can make us appear pretty pathetic in the fact that we are usually the last ones to know just how far forward we cannot go with our coping skills and thought processes until we attempt to move forward and can't.

2.

Adjusted focus determines how we repeat progress. Distorted focus determines how we repeat conflict.

It's access that your enemy eventually beats you with, not strength. New battles are rarely the result of new enemies more than the result of old doors the same enemies are still using to get to you.

➤ *Don't try to change other people's focus in order to protect your own.* We do this in order to not feel bad if our decisions disappoint anyone.

➤ *Don't apologize for your right to say no.*

➤ *Make decisions only from the track that the most productive you needs to follow.* If you don't, you will make decisions from the position of guilt at not being able to accommodate everyone else's track.

➤ *Do everything from a position of win-win.* You losing so someone else can win is not them abusing you; rather, it is you abusing yourself. Don't do that.

Even what seems to be sacrifice on behalf of your children is still a win-win for you if they grow up to be secure, strong, and respectable adults because of the good you sowed into them.

3.

Become more honest over why you may be lazy in parts of your character; you love the way that laziness permits you to deal passively and at times carnally with hurt and disappointment.

Having problems does not mean we are failures. But allowing the same problems to repeat themselves will cause you to fail. *Lazy character is not about things you cannot get over. It is about things you do not want to.*

So, it gives you the capacity to handle situations with excuses, control, vindictiveness, abuse, and most of all denial without having to demand of yourself that you will not use pain to cope with pain.

Remember: *It is impossible to procrastinate dealing with the things you are not aware of. You will only procrastinate what you are trying to remain in denial about.*

Where is your behavior or personal integrity off course with where you need to be in this area?

How would the person you want to be handle this area differently?

Leadership without enforced excellence is merely pain management.

16

NOTHING EVER CHANGES UNTIL YOU CHANGE HOW YOU ARE PARTICPATING WITH IT.

Our barometer for where we either live or don't live with healthy boundaries is most always revealed through our interactions with other humans. This is because of the reality that none of us can claim personal growth until what we consider to be growth can be proven as growth through how we deal with people.

Meaning, without other people involved for our sobriety, we just become victims of fantasy and good intention through isolation. Then we become exploited by the trust that we place in the changes that our inclusive perspective said were credible, but the relational us proved was not.

Boundaries do not change other people; they change us. Which is why the purpose of enforcing healthy boundaries is to relieve us of being control freaks.

This is also why putting up better boundaries will not be hard. Getting to the place of being sick and tired of what is insane, unproductive, or chaotic will be.

It is when something cannot be governed by a proper boundary that you will force it to measure up to your control while you live hostile over where it might not be measuring up.

In fact, healthy boundaries are what relieve us by releasing us from needing anything or anyone around us to be better before we can be. All human nature does this. Women need men to be different first, men need women to be different first. People need more money before they can start managing money better, people need a bigger gym before they can start losing weight, et cetera, and the cycle never stops.

CEO FACT:

Peace always requires a choice.

No, not the choice to sit on the floor and hum or chant while you find your happy place. It is rather the choice of, *"What am I going to do to stop being the victim of anything unstable?"*

Where we do not love order, we do not love ourselves. So, it is impossible to say that you love you, but then you tolerate everything that divides you.

This is also where hostility can manifest through everything from cranky moods, violent outbursts, calloused demeanor, cynical and isolated perspective, and victim sounding codependence. All the way to vice hungry alternative lifestyles.

And sadly, the average person approaches instability or chaos with the attitude of, *"What do I need to do to tame it instead of remove it."* The danger however is that to control instability you have to fit in with instability.

This is why for a time *The Jerry Springer Show* was the highest rated daytime talk show in America. Chaos amused so many people because many could relate in some way to it.

Most people are in fact tired of pain. But most people are not tired enough of their pain to risk dramatic changes that could take them to a healthier level of life that is beyond their pain.

So, people will make statements like, *"Yeah, but I've been sick and tired for quite a while now."* That is just code for, *"All I am is sick and tired. But when push comes to shove, I will just back down and stay sick and tired."*

Here is the reality in this: *We don't cooperate with change, change cooperates with us. Change is not something that we wait for. It is something that we lead.*

This is where you can hear the average person say things like, *"If they do this one more time, then I am out of here!"* Good luck. To these people, one more time becomes several more times.

No, this is not about driving a hard bargain with imperfect people or incomplete circumstances. Anything sick can become well, as long as both sides are committed to that. But this is where boundaries come in. *We do not just become right in our lives. We enforce right.* That is what a boundary is; *the strategical enforcement of what is right.*

So, enforcing better boundaries is as much an issue of self-honesty as it is self-articulation over the types of things you can no longer handle the same way.

Yes, that's right. You do have a right to refuse participation with repetitive chaos and abuse. And you cannot wait to rate abuse based on if it is abuse to someone else. But you will never know that until you stop trying to speak out to change the chaos or the abuse and start speaking out instead for what your own growth as a person can no longer facilitate about your part of it.

This is why better boundaries are never difficult because they are hard. They are difficult because most people assume that the difficulty lies in the boundary more than it does the faith and trust needed to erect them and then stand by them.

The myth about boundaries is that it takes strength to put them up. Not so. *It takes strength to have faith and trust.* Faith in what is right and trust that what is right will reward you beyond what you may lose that is deficient and what you will gain that is good.

CEO FACT:

Every right boundary that we enforce will almost always cost us something or someone wrong in our life that was only connected to us because of where we lacked healthy boundaries.

Every better boundary will cost us a wrong habit.

Every better boundary will cost us a defect in our behavior.

Every better boundary will cost us an incompetent part of our belief system.

Every better boundary will cost us an inappropriate relationship that insists on staying inappropriate. Every better boundary in our life will most assuredly cost us a carnal motive that we are using for our existence.

Boundaries are only the result of what we believe about ourselves. The purpose of proper boundaries is not to live superior. It is to live independent of anything or anyone that insists on being divisive or destructive.

So, boundaries are not to prevent us from being connected to imperfect people. They are what prevent us from feeling obligated to play games with other people's imperfections in order to stay connected.

Boundaries are not what we put up in our attempt to become perfect either. They are what we put up in order to not live as a hostage to our own imperfections.

Boundaries are not what we put up after we have controlled something or someone to turn out like we needed. They are what we put up after we realize that we cannot control anything without becoming abused, exhausted, and deceitful in the process.

That is what all control is for; *so we do not have to trust.* Trust in our destiny, trust in people, and trust in what is on the other side of the times when our destiny blindsides us, and people disappoint us.

So, we conduct ourselves with bad habits and perverted coping skills because fear has convinced us that excessive self-reliance is a strength more than a trap.

CEO FACT:

Our boundaries will only be as big as our threshold for the chaos and pain that we tolerate is small.

Absorbing the wrong things is what creates dependence on the wrong things. In other words, we will repeat destructive cycles and chaotic situations because of how much of our system has been built to handle.

So, where our system is built to handle internal sickness then we cannot help but require more sickness, despite the fact that we resent it, in order to maintain our system.

Unfortunately we learn this as children. Especially if we had to survive loss or abandonment early on, or even if we were raised in white-picket-fence America but as the *"good child."* Meaning, the child under the pressure to carry the dignity of the family's future on his/her shoulders.

So, by the time we reach adulthood, we can be so immune to such toxic doses of what is unhealthy or insane, that like a professional drinker, we do not even feel the warning signs of a buzz until the bar counter is filled with an array of empty glasses.

So, nothing destructive on a scale of one to ten even gets our attention until it is already at a seven or eight. Usually by that time, all hell has broken loose.

It's kind of like the guy who has to be hit four or five times before it really sinks in that he is in a fight.

That is what absorbing is; *making something unhealthy around you, a part of you.*

For example, just before any person with substance addictions either dies of an overdose or is forced to enter rehab because of coming too close to one, they all will describe to you the pattern of how much they were enlarging their threshold for handling either bigger doses of a drug or bigger doses of a drug mixed with bigger doses of alcohol. People even do this with eating disorders and prescription medicine. They enlarge their capacity to handle more of it. Chaos is no different.

Sadly, to a chronic absorber, healthy boundaries are seldom their first choice. Mostly they just wait until everything that they are trying to either control or at least coexist with for their favor breaks down. Then they will usually reach for some out of character or over-the-top means as a way to cry out against what fear has convinced them they are too inadequate to stop fitting in with.

CEO FACT:

It is only what is still broken in us that connects us to destructive situations and destructive people.

You cannot use unhealthy approaches to fill unhealed holes.

Personally, the most abusive people that I have fallen victim to were only a result of a desire for a level of love, leadership, and tenderness that I never received as a child. What I did not realize at the time was that healthy people who can give you love, leadership, and tenderness cannot be controlled to do so. And they will definitely not give it to you just to replace everyone else who didn't.

So, to fill my voids I controlled to get other people to be what they were not, while ultimately having to control the abuse of everything that they were.

Since other people cannot do to us what we are not already doing to ourselves, you will only attract relationships as healthy as you love yourself.

So, the average abused person repeatedly takes abuse because they commit abuse with themselves first. This is also why the common reply from angry, inferior people who accept abuse is always an ultimatum of *"what they are not going to allow anyone else do to them ever again."* That is as normal as it is immature. What would life be if our response was, *"I'm sorry but I don't treat myself this way, so why should I let you?"*

Unhealthy people do not care about what you keep saying that you are not going to take anymore. They will keep taking advantage of you right on through your whole tough guy speech. However, what unhealthy people cannot keep being inappropriate towards you over is the decency and dignity by which you treat yourself.

This is why divorce is such an easy out. It's just easier to leave a situation we don't like than it is to demand that we turn something around about ourselves that could very possibly turn around our situation.

Of course, this is assuming that both parties are committed to the same change. But, hurt often prevails in place of self-accountability. But know this. You can change anything around you as long as you are willing to change something in you first.

So, when we settle for unhealthy environments and unhealthy relationships what we are really saying is, *"I don't have anything better to give a healthier situation, because I do not really expect anything better from myself."*

CEO FACT:

Where walls self-destruct us, we assume they are being used to prevent bad things from coming in, when in reality they are protecting bad things from going out.

The opposite of boundaries are walls. *Boundaries are a memorial to a strength. Walls are only a memorial to a wound.*

Boundaries change who we are. Walls just try to change what the world around us is.

Walls are what we build in the attempt to keep out everything that we are afraid to take responsibility to change about ourselves or slam the door to.

So, there is a reason why destructive people do not work in my organization anymore; *they can't.* I am no longer a destructive leader.

No, I did not build a wall around me so thick so as to minimize future people's potential betrayal of me.

I simply stopped allowing wrong people around me because I stopped being a wrong leader. *None of us stop living what we despise, until we stop living what we are.*

Walls keep the new us from getting in because they protect the old us from getting out. This is because walls do not cut off our pain. They cut off our growth.

This is also why boundaries are the result of something that has been healed, whereas walls are only the result of what is still hurting.

So with our walls, while what is harmful may not get to us as quickly because of a well-constructed self-preservation system we have built over time, nothing unhealthy ever leaves us either.

The problem is that every time our walls do not work, only because any vault sooner or later can get cracked regardless of the complication of its security system. Then all we do is become more and more socially retarded, non-relational, and depleted because of everything we do to go back to the drawing board and construct a more self-absorbed wall.

So, a forty-year-old adult can function with a fifteen-year-old's emotional immaturity and play a fifteen-year-old's adolescent games. All because somewhere a wall was put up to protect something bad that later on was never torn down because of something good. One reason why our walls never get torn down is because of *what our walls are used for storing.*

In other words, anytime we open our mouths, every word, description, terminology, tone, and process of reason reflects everything we have either grown past or are still wounded in. *Hurting people use hurting terminology. Healed people use healed terminology. So, our presentation never lies. It always reveals the healed us or the hurting us.*

One reason is because healing and growth do not lie. Neither does unresolved pain. Our words always come from our spirit. They tell exactly where we are or are not on the journey of progress at our most current time.

And we can prorate our position in the journey through good intention as much as we would like. But the reality is that we will only speak and act from the place where we are either currently centered or still off balance.

This brings up the issue of storing what is spoiled.

For example, there is no such thing as a spoiled refrigerator. There is only the spoiled food that a refrigerator stores.

However, in our internal refrigerator what happens to stored hurt, just like forgotten spoiled food, is the odor eventually becomes too noticeable to be undetected.

But when food is first spoiled you have to open the refrigerator to even notice it. Meaning, you usually have to get close enough to the food to detect it. However, the more time that is devoted to the storage of it, the stronger the odor will become until you can detect it just from walking into the house. *When a refrigerator is allowed to store what is deteriorated then what is deteriorated is allowed to contaminate what is good.*

This is not about being bad people. But we become deficient people based on the bad that we store.

So, our deepest disappointments and wounds or traumatic experiences ferment over time, usually right into a bitter and desensitized state and usually mixed with moderate or overwhelming doses of faulty teaching.

So, like the Chinese take-out from last month that we forgot was in the fridge, it does not mean that it was not there getting more rancid by the moment.

All until the stench of it through our quirks, cynicism, and hang-ups becomes too noticeable to the world around us whom we assumed would never go into our fridge.

So anything that still stinks in our attitude or our outlook is just a sign of what is still stuck in our emotional refrigerator. So, some days we do not know just how much we have stored until we attempt to move forward and can't.

CEO FACT:

Whatever we make provision to stay deformed in us we will also make provision to stay deformed around us.

I was talking with a ministerial colleague of mine one day who was telling me of three separate divisive splits he had within his congregation in recent years.

A split is where one group of self-centered destructive people exploit a void of vision and leadership within their group. Only to power move against what is usually another group of self-centered, destructive people exploiting the same thing. Of course, while both parties believe they are justified for doing so and while the often passive pastor tries to keep the ship on course through his/her own lack of leadership.

The danger of my friend's story however was in how accepting he was of all of this as if somehow this just comes with the territory and it is somehow *"all the devil's fault."*

I told him that the first split could be blamed on what he did not know as a leader. But splits two and three could only be blamed on what he had refused to change as a leader.

I get this same scenario from women who tell me that they keep attracting brutal men. Or business owners who keep hiring fraudulent employees.

So, we leave an unfaithful relationship and say, *"I'm never going to love like that or give myself that much to another person again."* We call that a boundary. Well, it's not.

First of all, when you erect walls, you will only be protecting your own immaturity. Walls only make it possible for us to manage the fallout from our own delusion and arrogance.

Secondly, boundaries will connect you to other people with boundaries. Walls will just connect you to other people with walls. Boundaries are simply what we put up when we decide that we do not need to fix the past in order to fix ourselves.

The problem however when two walled people connect is that it is never about relationship. It is more about a brokered deal that we will place a relationship sticker on. Then it becomes about who can out-manipulate who the most to benefit their own personal walls.

So, this superficial negotiation that is called a relationship, and often times a marriage only exists on the premise that *"you protect my walls, and I will protect yours."* This is of course until the relationship falls apart because nothing good is left to get out of it because nothing healthy has been put into it.

And this is the deal. We are only able to maintain such a connection up until the place where we are forced to give something better than what is inside of our walls. Because for walled people, it is a game of seeing how much you can get, what can benefit you the most, without having to go beyond your walls to get it. Of course, all before having to move on to the next connection and repeat the same scenario.

1.

Clean the fridge.

How? Write down on paper everything that you notice that you do to manage the broken parts of you.

Cleaning the fridge is cleaning out all of the excuses that we have not to clean it. Meaning people do not leave spoiled food in their fridges because they have to, but because procrastination tells them they will remove it later.

Then you must clean out all of the good intentions that you have created for protecting what is in the fridge because you would rather believe that somehow month-old Chinese take-out should still be okay if you heat it up.

Secondly, list the things that you know you work to go along with, that you resent going along with, but you do so anyway. Either because of fear or a power trip you are playing with pain. *We cannot use the best of ourselves to manage the worst. Sooner or later there is nothing good left of us to manage.*

Thirdly, write down everything you notice that you do to control fear. How much pretending do you do to not notice the red flags that insanity and deception are throwing up?

How much do you shut down just to coexist with fear mostly because of what you would fear losing if you didn't?

Fourthly, list the things that you notice you do as responses to when other people attempt to hook you with your own frailties or mistakes.

Do you use integrity and self-decency to get out of the way? Or do you roll over and play dead just to get them to stop swinging?

Do you resort to foul play to swing back? Or, do you engage in secret things to self-medicate your passivity while you get displaced revenge on the situation?

Fifthly, list the excuses that you make to avoid the level of accountability with qualified people that could challenge you into a place of healing your deception thus changing your behavior.

These areas are where you are looking for agreement more than honesty. These areas are also areas where you only want to get *"accountable-acting"* after you believe you have fixed everything by yourself.

Sixthly, describe the logic your mind uses every time it talks you out of making the changes that you feel convicted to make in your broken areas, but you don't. You will know these areas because on the brink of finally putting your foot down for deep change, something about surface behavior modification throws you a bone of the situation appearing to get better.

So, then you back off from enforcing change, only to get re-setup for disappointment all over again.

Lastly, list the parts of your decisions that you are still making from a position of insecurity. All insecure motives in decision making are based on a void in us that we are trying to fill. The problem is that filling voids and solving the real problem are rarely the same thing.

2.

Anything that you want to remove, you will have to shrink your capacity to handle less of it.

Bad things only stay in our lives to the degree that we have been built to handle them.

➤ *React quicker when your awareness is telling you that you are at the same situations again.* Speak up about unhealthy things because it is right and not when you have stuffed so much you finally explode.

➤ *Interrupt negative cycles at a much sooner point.* It is only at this point that you will act on things while they are still a leak and not a flood.

➤ *Stop placing your focus on what other people do wrong and start placing it on what you do right.*

You will only minimize your threshold for pain at the pace that you are enlarging your threshold for loving yourself.

Loving you is about loving what is decent and sane. It only starts with choosing to believe that you are lovable and that your purpose in life matters.

3.

Any boundary worth its salt must be continually refined.

Healthy boundaries are never what we set and then leave. They are not the crockpot that can cook all day while you are at work. Every disappointment, miscalculation, and conflict that you will ever encounter will expose the pieces of a faulty boundary that you have.

Don't take it personal, just refine them. Healthy boundaries do not have a plateau to them. So don't try to set one.

Where is your behavior or personal integrity off course with where you need to be in this area?

How would the person you want to be handle this area differently?

Leadership is rarely about your ability to bring change. It is more about your willingness not to wait for others to bring it.

17

YOUR PROGRESS WILL BE AS MUCH YOUR WILLINGNESS TO WALK AWAY FROM WHAT IS OLD, AS IT WILL BE YOUR WILLINGNESS TO WALK TOWARDS WHAT IS NEW.

Anyone can say they are ready for new beginnings in something. But not everyone can walk away from something old to embrace them.

So, when it comes to stepping up to master seasons of transition in your life one reality holds true: *people do not have a problem with a better place in life they cannot seem to get to. They have a problem with everything old and unproductive that they keep trying to take to a better place.*

One reason for this is the battle to acknowledge what is expired, or no longer healthy, that we either are unaware that is or we wished wasn't.

So, our steps forward become immobilized by carrying what we wished was different rather than motivated by what we are embracing that is actually different.

So, on the brink of a new level certain mediocrities and hang-ups that you had the tolerance to carry up to your current point, now become much too heavy to deny their existence. It is at this point that some unproductive behavior and some unhealthy people either get removed or they change along with you.

CEO FACT:

Increased stress will simply mean that you are getting closer to what is impossible to keep doing the same way anymore.

Anything outdated is a vehicle for pain. And to maintain anything outdated will require you to use outdated coping skills to do it.

It's like this: Some days we carry things because we either have had the strength or the ignorance to. So the moment those things must either be matured or removed, the ability to carry them in their current state will begin to wane.

This does not necessarily mean that something is bad. Some things do not have to be bad to be over . . . they just have to be expired in the purpose they were meant to facilitate. This also does not mean that someone close is going to leave you. It just means that something that has facilitated yesterday or even today, has to change because it cannot facilitate tomorrow the same way.

CEO FACT:

The greatest decisions to change anything can only be made from a singular position.

All change has nothing to do with who gets on board with it. It only has to do with the singular decisions you are willing to make because of the person you want to be. So, the decision to succeed cannot even be made until you can stop carrying who or what you are hoping will change, before you give yourself permission to change.

Most people don't make singular decisions for change. They make *"train decisions."*

A train decision is when we identify all of the cars we have to hook up to us and pull before we can ever get in the driver's seat and go.

That is what a singular decision is: *making decisions for your own personal change based on the purpose you are called to carry out and the kind of healthy and fulfilling lifestyle you are called to live.*

Making singular decisions means making decisions for your personal improvements and life direction FOR YOURSELF AND BY YOURSELF AND REGARDLESS OF WHO OR WHAT ELSE CHANGES OR NOT!

This is why most people don't make them. What they make is limited decisions just after they have succeeded at controlling everyone and every resource in their inner circle to get on board and change too. Or at the very least after they have been able to guarantee that they won't be rejected, judged, and abandoned if they are to make such decisions.

One reason is because so much of our self-worth is wrapped up in who gets on board with the improvements we are convicted to make, that we never really get on board. All of our time is spent manipulating on various levels like a Capitol Hill lobbyist in order to get the rest of the cars attached before we can start the train.

Then we get enraged the moment we are slapped with the reality that what has not changed after our continual Oscar nominated performances and our sugar coated deviousness has tried to coax it to change, was really never going to change at all.

Yes, our decisions most certainly affect other people in some way always. And no, singular decisions are not our cue to become masters at selfishness. However, *you cannot carry people or circumstances into every decision for personal change before you make it.*

Shame and fear will do this when it convinces you that you need to reason with what needs changing before you change it. But getting free is about changing you in order to change the kinds of things you keep participating in. So your decisions have nothing to do with who, or what, is around you that needs improving. They only have to do with you.

For example, in my church in Minneapolis I taught a series entitled *Taking Back Your Power.* This title will also be a forthcoming book of mine in the near future.

In the series I pointed out that one of the greatest secrets of taking back our personal power, since we only live at our most helpless and unhealthy state where we feel powerless, is to *"shrink the number of things that you carry."*

Meaning, most people only attempt to change *what* they carry rather than *why* they carry it.

So, in the process of making singular decisions for personal change, you cannot allow the decision to be a better you to be based on the hope that other people will want to be a better them.

We fall victim to this because of the shame of trying to be people pleasers. Really it is just the pride of assuming that we could please everyone coupled with the lack of self-worth to even want to try.

CEO FACT:

When a season of life is over, you will have to let go of the disappointment from the things that did not go the way that you thought they would or believed they should. That can now be used as a vehicle of offense to distort the next season where you are going.

Some seasons end with more questions than answers and for the moment more disappointments than victories.

Some seasons can change in ways that we could not even see coming while we crawl around like a stunned fighter trying to find the ropes to pull ourselves up with.

The only reason why we underestimate how a particular season of life may close is because we usually underestimate the kinds of things that cannot continue any further.

In other words, we just assume that certain dysfunction or disorder or even temporal parts of us that we had grown accustomed to dragging through several other seasons of life, now can just be dragged into another one. Then we find out that they can't.

However, what we will not push through in our own disappointments from yesterday, will just serve as the anger for us cursing our new seasons based on the letdown of our old ones.

To not fall victim to this we have to agree to let go of what did not end the way that we wanted it to or thought it should, lest we stay someplace expired. Of course, while we attempt to juggle the pain from trying to turn things around that cannot be turned around in their current state.

So, unfortunately, moving forward in anything has nothing to do with the absence of pain, but rather the presence of understanding. And you will never move on in anything where you are not willing to replace a blind spot in you first. A blind spot is either the evolvement of an unhealed wound or the existence of an unchallenged belief system. Either way your own blind spots can always abort what your greatest enemies never would be able to.

Like a corporate CEO who wants to blame a fraudulent employee when in reality that CEO hired them. Or the wife who kept venting to me one day about what an idiot her husband was. Of course, until I pointed out to her that she chose him.

You can hear it on a daily basis in people's attitudes and vocabulary; *where they fell down months ago or years ago, but in their outlook and their coping skills they still function like they just fell down yesterday.*

And there is something about trying to rebuild yesterday; *we have to be the same people we were yesterday to do it.*

And unfortunately our blind spots are never dealt with until something bad that we believe cannot produce something good that we cannot live without.

The truth be told, none of us really have difficulty moving through transitional or anxious times.

Our problem is with the difficulty of wanting to see things differently enough to move on, which is also where our paradigms have been built for safety more than reality.

Meaning, where any of us have constructed a belief system that does more to protect us from reality than accurately depict reality to us.

Even sensitive issues like the loss of a loved one or friend, while certainly not in every case, but in some, we have trouble getting over our losses. Only because of how much we are really having trouble seeing the reality of what may have facilitated the loss in the first place.

CEO FACT:

Never give CPR to anything that God is allowing to die.

In transition, warfare is not always the sign that something expired is leaving. It can also be the sign that you are fighting for something expired to stay. So, it becomes impossible to move on from anything unnecessary that you are babysitting.

And it is fairly easy to know when something is dying either because the purpose for what it was needed for is over or the favor to facilitate it in its current state is lifting. Either way, you can discover this in advance and move forward with it, or you can discover this abruptly when your own control blows up in your face.

This is when you have one choice. Let an outdated way of doing things die so a healthier way of doing things can resurrect, or live or deal with the stress of dragging the old you around in its dead state.

Either way, *you will know when something is dying because the pressure is magnified to keep it alive.*

We do this because yesterday has not yielded the results or answers that we believed they were supposed to yet. No, this is not to say that if your marriage is dead, then get rid of it and find someone else. But the old and unhealthy ways of doing things need not be dragged along on your life-support system just because you believe things should be different.

1.

Let go of the disappointment from unrealistic expectations and unrealistic goals.

There will be seasons that end unlike you wanted them to. However, you will not begin a new season right with resentment more than wisdom.

We do not get to ask why a season ended as much as we get to decide if we are going to begin a new one differently by how accurately we are willing to restructure our reality.

Reality never lies to us about anything. We lie to ourselves about reality. So every time a piece of your understanding enlarges in something a piece of what is only fantasy has to be removed.

➤ *Don't be so married to a plan that you cannot restructure it when you keep falling short of your goal.* Having a plan is not the problem. Having a plan that your stubbornness cannot redirect is.

In transitional times, right opportunities will not always line up with your ideas. So, it would be better to redirect your steps more than repair them.

2.

Let go of the disappointment from what was maybe not wrong purpose but rather wrong timing.

According to Solomon's teaching, all purposes have timing to it (see Ecclesiastes 3). So, anytime you take something beyond the boundaries of timing, you force it to survive without the strength of purpose. And anything that the timing of purpose is not required to sustain . . . you will have to.

3.

Let the temporary bless you as the temporary and let the permanent develop to be the permanent.

Human nature always wants to place the *"forever"* tag on anything or anyone who has been good to us.

It's the logic of *"why would anything just be good only for a time and then move on?"*

What you are given to start a season will not always be what you are given to end one. So, what God uses to get you off the ground will not always be what He uses to keep you in the air.

Some days one right temporary person can remove a lot of wrong permanent problems. And you can only tell the difference by looking at the types of decisions someone makes to establish credible foundation versus just solve a now problem. Either way learn to celebrate both.

Remember: anything temporary or permanent reveals itself because of what it is, not because of what you make it.

4.

Where and with whom can't you be the new you with?

Never try to speculate who yesterday people are.

A healthier you will automatically place distance between you and anyone who is still an unhealthy them.

That is the issue about old relationships; *not history, but old patterns*. That is how you identify yesterday people. They keep making it easier for you to be the old you.

They will also never allow you to forget when the old you disappointed them. That is because they are still the old them.

Where is your behavior or personal integrity off course with where you need to be in this area?

____

____

____

____

____

____

____

How would the person you want to be handle this area differently?

____

____

____

____

____

____

____

Leadership is only advanced by the depth you can draw from other people while not needing to become them to do it.

18

THE SALE OF YOUR INDEPENDENCE IS THE LAST STEP BEFORE OBSCURITY.

It is kind of hard to imagine the concept of human nature that one could sell their independence much like one could sell a used car or vacuum cleaners. But the issue exists nonetheless in what we do on a daily life basis from a position of helplessness and powerlessness to trade pieces of our identity, morality, and purpose. All in exchange for being liked, minimizing rejection, and manipulating emotional safety.

Married couples do this to survive issues of control and domination or when core needs go unmet.

Family members do this to survive an abusive parent, sibling, et cetera. Corporate people do this to survive in power abusive companies. Cabinet members do this to survive in fraudulent government regimes. We who do, or have done, this on any level do it for the same reason—*to fit in with what we fear we cannot change.* Change about the people or circumstances we fear may never like us, value us, accept us, or understand us enough.

So, we agree to trade a piece of ourselves to facilitate situations that can only be resolved through the defense of what is decent rather than the denial of what is not.

We attempt to do so by bartering with values that cannot be bartered with, only to wonder down the road, *"Where did we lose ourselves?"* When in reality, the moment you gave away values because you opted not to defend your values, you gave away you.

That is the deception. Where we believe that we have to trade parts of ourselves in order to change the things that we really do not have to change, we just have to love ourselves enough instead to not keep facilitating them. But that would be the easy thing to do, and most days in a powerless existence, easy is the hardest to recognize.

One reason we don't initially take this approach is because where we do not know enough of ourselves, our coping mechanisms are built more for survival than personal integrity. Especially in abusive or threatening situations.

So, the goal at the time is as noble as it is distorted in that if we can purchase a false peace, then that is better than living with the void of any peace at all.

The problem is that false peace is like a spare tire. It can get you a few miles down the road until you are forced once again to deal with the reality of what your real tire problem is.

CEO FACT:

Most people live between the extremes of independent versus codependent, with no middle ground in between. The middle ground is interdependent.

This meaning, the place where we can draw from the contributions of everyone without losing ourselves in the process.

Interdependent is the place where we are not forced to participate with everything that is not supposed to be us, just so we can be us.

Interdependent is also the place of not having to be so independent that we avoid intimacy and accountability, or so codependent that we live desperate for the right people to own us. Without interdependence all we will do is live independent as our way of making sure we never experience the pain of when we used to be codependent ever again.

This is one reason the average person does not understand confidence. *Confidence is the freedom to be you without needing to sell you. It is when you sell you that you will live with the fear of who may not be buying or the regret of who did.*

People struggle with confidence when their drive to achieve their dreams and goals is smaller than their need for just being liked for having some. So, the only thing worse than not having a dream because of a lack of vision, is trying to sell your dream because of a lack of confidence.

Sometimes you will never know that you are impressionable enough to be controlled until you see where you have exchanged compromised loyalty for conditional favor.

So if you are going to be exploited for having a lack of identity, this will usually be the chain of command of sorts in how it works.

The first step of a controlling person will be to empower your hang-ups via your hurts and unmet needs.

The second step will be to dull your edge by selling you a version of independence that is void of identity. Which really means it is just codependence infused with superficiality.

The third step will be to appeal to your fear of failure or rejection so that you will trade being affirmed for being used.

CEO FACT:

We can never become healthy people until we agree to get delivered from the fear of being codependent on who, or what, we believe has the power to make us or break us.

What we choose to handle through codependence only prevents bad people, bad habits, and bad behavior from leaving us.

Codependence has its own insanity in that it resents pain but fears letting go of what causes it.

So, a woman being sexually harassed by her boss can resent it, but nevertheless can keep tolerating it because she fears what may happen to her career or income if she stands up to it. One spouse can resent the other spouse's abuse or infidelity but keeps tolerating it because they either fear being alone or starting over alone.

This is one reason why fear is so powerful. While it cannot make you do anything, it can convince you to do everything.

So, when it comes to conquering fear, we can only rate progress in our lives by what we are doing to trust decency more than fear conflict.

And at the end of the day, there is only one definition of success: HAVING ENOUGH OF WHAT YOU NEED INTERNALLY TO BE ABLE TO REFUSE ENOUGH OF WHAT YOU SHOULD NOT HAVE TO PARTICIPATE WITH EXTERNALLY IN ORDER TO SUCCEED.

Men who are gripped by the fear that their wives might cheat on them. Women gripped by fear of losing their appeal to a man and being replaced.

Personally, I even relate with colleagues on the church side of my occupation that are always on guard against what their denomination could take from them if a rumor or personal crisis were to become too uncontrollable. *We only lose what we fear that other people or other circumstances have the capacity to take from us.*

No, this is not to say that any of us should start singing the *"I don't need anyone anymore"* martyrs' national anthem. But it is to say that at whichever point we stop in life it is only because of what fear said had the capacity to stop us that has now become the center of our life.

So, when one person's rejection of us stops us, then their rejection has become our life.

When one setback stops us, then that setback has become our life. When one divorce stops us, or one business flop or one miscarriage stops us, then any of those disappointments have become our life.

And where we stop, it is never where we are forced to, but rather where we agree to. Then we are forced to develop coping mechanisms to stay where we are by accepting where we are. Which means, we have to use superficiality to put a positive spin on who or what we are attempting to rescue in order to sell it to ourselves first and then to anyone who may see through it.

CEO FACT:

You will never achieve a goal better than how you see yourself.

The ability to love the wrong things about you is not self-esteem. It is self-deception.

Quote all the daily affirmations you want, but you and I will never reach for anything better that what we choose to believe about ourselves.

That's just it; *we will only give away personal power in the areas where we are unwilling to enforce personal decency.* So when it comes to the fear of loss in enforcing healthy personal boundaries *you will never lose anything for the right reasons that can take you forward. Anything we lose for the right reasons are only the things that can digress us.*

And you will know an unhealthy self-image because it involves the performance of attitude and presentation to cover for the insecurity of unresolved pain and underdeveloped identity we feel obligated to outperform.

So, using our esteem for performance or self-protection just means we have no esteem at all. We have *self-allusion.* Self-allusion only produces attitude more than answers. Answers produce contentment whereas attitude only masquerades a lack of answers.

Bad esteem however is only the result of believing lies about yourself. And none of us will ever go further in life than the inaccuracies that we choose to believe about ourselves.

Positive esteem is not when we can put positive spins on the worst parts of us. Rather, it is the protection of our own self-decency.

So we only attempt to spin bad esteem when we are trying to cover up for pain we are absorbing rather than growing beyond. It's like, *"Hi, I used to be a size six, now I am a size sixty, but I am finally accepting myself."* Or, *"Hi, I abandoned my children and threw prosperous opportunities to the wind, but I feel as though I am finally learning to love me."*

Personally, I watch people make decisions that do more to dry them up on the inside than flourish them. But when you see them they will make the deterioration sound like it was the best decision they have ever made.

So, our deception becomes our self-esteem. Then we use what is external to sell the new us, when in reality it is still the hurting us. And while it is a fact that all things abusive can leave us feeling ugly, unworthy, and unprotected, healthy esteem cannot be described as the ability to coexist with the damage by sounding positive about it. We cannot describe calloused coping skills as somehow being what we consider part of our competency and positive skill.

It is also through bad esteem that we will punish a part of ourselves to cope with pain and to reduce how many people may want to hurt us again. It's like, *"If I hurt you before you hurt me, then I can minimize who hurts me by only attracting either the people who I can control, or the people who will expect less from me."*

CEO FACT:

Your identity will never be in your culture or your skills, but in the assignment of what you are put here on earth to affect.

Your assignment does not know color. It does not know background. It does not know difficulty. It only knows assignment.

One reason is because the solution that God could use you to be to someone else, does not have a color to it either. Only because pain does not know color; it only knows pain. Furthermore, where your esteem is not governed by your assignment, then where you have messed it up or where other people have rejected it will govern you instead.

1.

Remove the safety nets you have built for failure and loss.

You will never conquer what you give yourself convenient escapes to avoid. All that safety nets do is facilitate you living as an underachiever rather than a risk taker.

Safety nets get put into place so that we can trust ourselves to cope with the fallout from a level of failure that we have prepared to accept.

For example, the safety net of mediocrity. Meaning, if I run an area of my life low enough, then all it will cost me to protect myself from experiencing big letdowns will be the pressure to manage chaos and indecision.

Or bad esteem. Meaning, if I lower my standard then I lower my risk of rejection. So, while all I will really attract are the destructive, the helpless, the shallow, and the socially retarded, who cares? At least trying to fix abusive or other underachieving people gives me something to feel important about.

Or self-destruction. Meaning, if I hurt it before it hurts me, then regardless of the damage from being so self-centered that my life is now placed on hold to clean up, I am still in control.

And while I will still grieve over the quality of relationships that continually reject me, at least I have succeeded at not having to become healed enough to be relational. Of course, I will spin it by blaming the higher level of people who would not accept my mediocrity as *"them not loving me for who I am."*

Or chameleon. Meaning, if I become whatever to fit in wherever, then I will not be judged for not being a leader because no one will see me as one. Even though I will live off of everyone else's power, I still have managed to avoid being the one to step up and take on the giants. Besides, remaining shallow means that I am rarely judged.

2.

Don't use displaced methods to deal with direct problems.

Displaced methods prevent us from having to have enough faith in right decisions. They allow us the window to manipulate reality and at times allow people to be the masquerade for where we are living without enough security in a standard of personal decency to make right decisions.

It's like a single woman I knew who kept craving love and marriage with the right man. But when the single men she would date did not turn out to be right, she would resort to affairs with married ones.

Fear makes us do this. The fear of what may not work out like we want it to if we were to deal with it directly, mixed with the constant nagging discomfort of what we know cannot continue to stay the way it is.

3.

Where do you assume that unhealthy arrogance is the same as healthy esteem?

I was talking with a single woman on her quest of finding a quality man for a quality relationship.

She was quick to point out to me all of the wonderful things about her that in her words, *"most men could not handle."*

I was quick to point back to her that it was possible that there might be something about her that most men have no desire to handle. Her arrogance was just a reflection of both her inferiority and her unresolved anger towards past male relationships.

This is where people will put labels of confidence on insecurity. In other words, *"If you got it, then why beat around the bush about it."* It is actually a false confidence, which uses arrogance to mask fear. Don't be like that. People will gravitate towards what you have, not what you convince them you have.

Where is your behavior or personal integrity off course with where you need to be in this area?

How would the person you want to be handle this area differently?

Leadership never works in hiding.

19

YOU WILL NEVER BE ADDICTED TO A SUBSTANCE OR A VICE AS DESTRUCTIVE AS PASSIVITY.

Addictions are never a person's stronghold. They are merely the passive approach to ease the pain of the fear and anger that is really at the core of what would be a person's stronghold.

That is what addictions and vices are; *they are the wrappers we use to console the person we regret that we are, while we hide the person we are created to be, but are afraid to be.* So, ultimately the only thing we use addictions for is *to medicate a past that we hate or a future that we are afraid of.*

As people go, none of us are ever controlled by vices. We are only controlled by the passivity of what we will not do to take proactive steps to forgive, release, and strengthen within ourselves. To grow beyond injustices that fear has exploited our helplessness towards.

It's where we use self-destruction rather than self-improvement to take back personal power.

So, addictions are what we develop to coexist with the traps that fear has convinced us we are not strong enough, smart enough, or resourceful enough to live without. Then we sink deeper in self-deception by blaming a vice, like alcoholism or any other *"holism,"* on a disease. When is reality, passivity is the only decease. It is never in a bottle, a drug, a food binge, or an internet porn sight.

Yes, too much dependence on something addictive can create an addictive pattern. However, vices just ease the pressure of how hard it is to perform as broken people as if we were really whole. So, we mask our refusal to get tough about personal pain behind a terminology that portrays a vice as having a power that it has never had. Veiled, of course, in a terminology that derives more sympathy than personal responsibility.

Then we go to twelve-step programs whose whole beginning statement to their recovery mantra is, *"We are powerless to this disease."* Yippee. Let's all just go home and die. *You cannot conquer anything you feel powerless to. Powerlessness is what gets you addicted to a vice in the first place. So, you cannot use what gets you hooked to get you unhooked.*

Powerlessness does not provoke the freedom of anything. It only provokes the definite co-existence with it while we attempt to manage a life without bondage, while managing the bondage. And fear makes people feel powerless, not alcohol. The worthlessness from injustices makes people feel powerless, not cocaine. So, the recovery process can never be about trying to manage the escapes.

So, our fights with any addiction become based simply on the level of honesty we are afraid to see about what the fight really is versus what we have tried to turn the fight into. Mixed of course with the fear of what we may not be able to control about the outcome.

So, alcohol, cocaine, food binging, throwing up food, gambling, or extramarital affairs are like the friend we bring into the fight because of the fighter we are afraid to be by ourselves.

And with addictions we are never medicating what we cannot grow past as much as what we resent that we should even have to. In other words, some of the fights we are now forced as adults to deal with should never have even been our fights.

So, in reality we are medicating the duty of the process. We are medicating the person we are afraid to be or resent being expected to be and not the person we are.

It's the syndrome of, *"I did not ask for this pain, then why should I have to be the one to make dramatic changes to grow bigger than it?"* So, passivity is brought in instead to blame the pain of growing up on a disease supposedly found in a bottle.

CEO FACT:

Truth is not brutal. How much we are living without truth is.

People will use terms like *"brutal truth or brutal honesty."* Those terms are not so realistic.

Or they attribute directness to a person's personality trait with statements like, *"They can really tell it like it is."* That is not true either. *The discovery of truth is never brutal. The discovery of how much we have been deceived is.*

Truth only rocks us in places because deception hasn't rocked us enough. It is only where we are not lovers of truth that directness offends us.

Where the direct approach is concerned, *directness is not the fruit of personality. It is the fruit of truth. It is not that people get offended at directness. They just get offended over what directness does not allow them to hide.*

Directness with love and respect should be your norm of relating in your inner circle.

Directness is not arrogance either. Arrogance is insecurity. Directness is clarity. When someone accuses clarity of being rude, usually they are just uncomfortable at what they are forced to see.

Besides, it would be better for someone to be mad at you and know where they stand with you than it would be for them to like you and assume they are standing some place they are not.

CEO FACT:

You only get what you build for.

- A corporation that experiences a takeover.
- A government that experiences a coup.
- A church that experiences a split.
- A marriage that experiences a divorce.

What do all of these things have in common? They were all built to experience what they went through.

Power giant, Enron, could fall because of what was in it's foundation to fall. As respectfully as I can say this, America fell for a tragic moment on September 11, 2001 at the hands of terrorism because at that time in our homeland security we were built to fall.

No, this is not an issue of you get what you deserve. But no change is ever a reliable change until it changes something in your foundation first. The behavior modifications that we want to pass off as change are only just that—*behavior modifications.* They are the band-aids we place on problems in route to dealing with what is at the root of the problem. The danger is when we attempt to solve foundational problems with a modification.

Anything that a leader reaps, good or bad, will be the result of what was sown into the foundation by that leader that could produce it.

Your spending habits, eating habits, relationships, coping skills, recovery mechanisms, anything that experiences growth was built for growth. Anything that experiences division was built for division.

The destructive can only work when something destructive is built into it to facilitate it.

So, what can divide you is only the result of what was built to divide you. And you will never effectively lead yourself where your tolerance for what can divide you cannot protect you.

CEO FACT:

Great visionaries are not determined by what they have an idea for but rather what they have a depth for. So, where you will not take your limitations seriously enough you will eventually shrink everything around you to the level of your limitations.

Depth is not something you learn. It is something you change for. The depth of a leader simply means that in everything you are big or small as a person, you will turn everything around you into.

For example, take a leader with the capacity for something great and give him/her something average and they will multiply it until it is what it they are. Give a leader with the capacity for something mediocre something great and they will deplete it until it is reduced to less than what it could be just so it can better fit them.

Thus is the trap of being a leader with limited depth; *you also have built in coping mechanisms to remain limited.*

And this is where all limitations come from; *the bad teachers and the bad experiences we have never outgrown.* So, in the case of a shallow depth leader, he/she will reduce something bigger than them down until it is smaller than them. Not so they can control vision, but so they control fear. No, not the fear of failure, but the fear of bigger. Failure is never what we fear. Being successful is.

So, it's not that uncommon leaders believe they are going to be more successful than everyone else. It's just that they are not afraid to be. This is because their vision is big enough to learn from their failures and their identity is not in what others think of them as a result of failing.

CEO FACT:

You will never bounce back quickly in anything without knowing the difference between sobriety and shame.

This is the other arena of where our passivity exploits the difference between where we change to overcome obstacles versus just personalize the fact that we even have some; *the issue of shame versus sobriety.*

This is also where our setbacks gain access to contaminate the sobriety process by when it ceases to be sobriety, and becomes part emotional mutilation and another part denial ridden shock.

This is why shame, while deadly, is also arrogant. One reason is because *there is no shame in sobriety. There is only shame in denial.* Shame is really just the arrogance that assumes that our character defects could never want to do the bad things that they really want to do. Accompanied also, by the ignorance to believe that we could ever be our own best support system when they do. And therein lies the shock value. The part where we want to act so overwhelmed at how our selfish dark parts could ever act out in ways so selfish and so dark.

The part where we want to talk in total clueless, but arrogant terms, like, *"I can't believe I did that; that's just not me."* Or, *"It was like I was a whole other person."*

And of course, after shock comes the embarrassment phase which is really just false pride. No, not embarrassment over what we did, but more of an embarrassment towards where our own denial exploited us. A self-betrayal if you will. Then there is the anger phase. No, not the anger of restlessness to change . . . but more often the anger towards who may not be as shocked at our behavior than we want to be.

And, yes, on the surface shame has the unmistakable feelings like the condemnation of *"You've lost, and you're not worthy.* Or, *you've messed it up again."*

But this worthlessness is really only a *false sorrow* which acts to consume, and at times, enamor you with what you did, rather than convict you to change why you did it. *Shame regardless of how bad we can feel is really just the enchantment with mistakes.*

Shame can only remind you of what you've done. It cannot sober you to who you are.

Shame is also the agreement we make to absorb and carry the situations that our lack of self-respect or self-morality repeatedly lands us in. And none of us can improve because we see what we've done . . . we can only improve because we see who we are.

And shame is only the result of getting caught, not getting aware. Shame is not the same as guilt. Guilt is where we know we have failed at not embracing the convictions to change. But shame is just the narcissism of wanting to feel bad about being betrayed by everything that we already knew could cause problems because we were not changing it.

And how do you stay out of shame? Well, besides getting over any talent for knowing how to play dumb about your mistakes so you can avoid being honest about them, I would also recommend that you to *stay out of remorse*.

Shame can only work where you are living in secret about yourself. *Shame protects secrets. And all sickness can only live in secret.* So with shame we only do things to position us as being better people than the ones we feel like because of our mistakes.

And all that remorse does is allow us to reflect on the things we want to feel sorry for more than change. And feeling sorry for what we do does not mean that we change our character. It just means that we are sorry at what our lack of character has cost us.

Remember two things:

1. You will only repeat the same type of conflicts for the same reasons.

People are only ashamed of their past because of how many things in their present are still the same. So, you can self-destruct in ten jobs and four marriages, but it will always be for one repetitive reason. And until you change your reasons you will never change what you keep encountering.

2. When you are desperate enough for solutions, how you look for having problems will not matter.

You will only master the problems that you are not so consumed with how you look for having them.

So, where you wrestle with what looks too big to get over, you are really wrestling with sobriety instead. Meaning, you would rather spend your time being overwhelmed or mad than aware.

1.

Don't practice situational integrity.

Instant change is not what we get to claim the moment we have been burned by the very disorder we have promoted.

I completely understand that some of our most dramatic life changes can be the result of overnight moments of eye-opening experiences. I also wholeheartedly concur with my own principle that some days it takes the evil against us to burn out the evil in us.

Of course, it's always easiest to get righteous just after we get embarrassed. The point is that *the game of dysfunction is always the game of dysfunction even before we get made a fool by it. So to become healthier people at no time can we claim instant morality just because the immoral games that we can sometimes play now have played us.*

Anything compromised in us only robs us. It does not prosper us. Yes, success costs, but dysfunction and perversion cost more.

And unfortunately, this is the selfish side of human nature that we use purposed passivity to tame the guilt of noticing our own double standards in.

The double standard where we do not react with conviction to inappropriate and abusive issues of life, much less issues that are a gross negligence towards what is truth, until we are the ones being victimized by them.

People do this at work. They sit in the coffee gossip cliques and discuss the boss they don't like, the company policies they resent, and the new employees who are not in the clique.

With no conviction of what it means to be a positive and dedicated leader within the company who signs their checks, despite what may be lacking in the company. And with no clue as to the destructive force of strife.

Then one day, BOOM! They are the ones being gossiped about or betrayed. Then it becomes an issue of how bad gossip is in the workplace and "can you believe the attitudes of these people," et cetera. *A difference in overall principle is what separates us from anyone, not a difference in chemistry. So, you cannot hate wrong only when it is being done to you. And you cannot justify passivity all in the name of, "It's not my war."*

Personally, when I went through a divorce in 2004, what became more of a shock to me than the actual reality that my then wife may have been planning to leave for some time was how many of our shared family and so-called friends immediately went silent. I would sit and tell myself that any moment now these people are going to step in, invited or not, and help me fight to keep something together that did not need to be divided.

I've heard all the arguments of, *"Well maybe they weren't asked, or they thought that you did not want their help. Or maybe they wanted to just give you and your wife the space to handle your own business."*

Part of the grief that it took me months to work through was a combination of three perspectives that had in different ways produced the silence of these same people that would also ultimately change how I would respond to other people in need.

1. With some their lack of response was a presumed safety of wanting to believe that this type of situation would never happen to them.

2. With others it was an underlying fear of where their own relationships were not that far out of reach of being in the same situation. So, better to be silent and let sleeping dogs lie.

Remember: *People never come to the aid of what they are afraid of. They only judge or avoid what they are afraid of. People only defend what they are healthy in.*

3. People cannot give you what is not in them.

You and I will never fight for anything beyond the current depth that we are or are not as individuals. So, you cannot expect people to help you on a level beyond anything mediocre they have accepted in their own lives.

Thus are the rewards of situational integrity. Situational morality is for the purpose of not having to pick a side. Truth never defends a person. It only defends a side.

➤ *You cannot assume that a problem is only a problem when you are the one having it.*

Imagine this type of thinking if we were to witness a person caught in a serious car accident in front of our very own eyes. Imagine us telling the cops, *"They did not ask us to help,"* or *"I just wanted to give them the space to call 911 themselves."*

No, you can't solve every problem or convince every person to always do the right thing. But the point is this: *You don't always fight for what is right because someone invites you to or gives you permission to. And you don't just get moral only when you are the hunted.*

Besides, you have nothing to lose if you are rejected for speaking out.

2.

Can your current level of personal ethics and integrity produce the next level of prosperity you desire?

A lot of times we do not even know what is perverted until we can no longer handle the damage from what is perverted anymore.

Thus, the other great blind spot of human nature; *when we believe that we deserve more prosperity and success in life than we believe that we should have to upgrade about our personal value system to produce.*

One cannot look at the issue of staying out of the trap of practicing situational morality as mentioned above, without also looking at where the code they function by is producing more disappointments than victories, more deterioration than growth.

➤ *Change your standard of integrity and your code of leadership ethics and you will change your prosperity level.* Nothing you put your hand to can flourish beyond the code of ethics and values that you currently practice.

Even in the midst of some of my own roughest seasons of life I would watch more people then I would have ever assumed around me get passive, distant, cold, two-faced, prejudiced, and most of all uninvolved. But what shocked me about these same people was what I saw in many of them later. *Unnecessary conflict directly associated to the complete void of personal excellence that they portrayed.*

I could not stay mad at them because quickly I realized that this is the way they handle life with everyone.

Eventually when many of these types of people *"just don't get it,"* they finally turn on each other.

Where is your behavior or personal integrity off course with where you need to be in this area?

____

____

____

____

____

____

____

How would the person you want to be handle this area differently?

____

____

____

____

____

____

____

Leadership is the ability to teach people how to apply your solutions, not teach them how to carry your blind spots.

20

HOW WE ACHIEVE SUCCESS IS AN ISSUE OF DETERMINATION. HOW WE MAINTAIN SUCCESS IS AN ISSUE OF HOW MUCH WE ALLOW UN-IMPRESSIONABLE PEOPLE TO IRRITATE THE HELL OUT OF OUR OWN SELF-DECEPTION.

Accountability is not so that you can confess your sins. It is so that you can save yourself from having to lie about what makes you sin. This explains the definition of failure. Failure is never the result of what others believe inaccurately about you. Rather, it is the result of what you believe inaccurately about yourself. And let's understand one thing. Self-deception can wear a three thousand dollar suit and fly on a private jet as easily as it can go in and out of jail for petty crimes.

That being said, in every season of life there is always a piece of your most successful and transforming changes that can only be made based on what someone else sees, not what you see.

This is because none of us fail in life where other people are deceived. We fail where we are. We don't follow the wrong kinds of leaders into a ditch because the leader is blind. We follow because we are.

I watch leaders who fall or who live destructively in their professional and/or personal lives. What I never see at the time of their decline is anyone around them screaming for change in their lives.

Why? The instinctive flawed response of all human nature. The reality that when any of us gets ready to choose failure over success, simply by choosing self-deception over what is truth, we make sure that we alienate ourselves just enough from anyone who has too much integrity to validate us choosing self-gratification over self-responsibility and personal pain over principle.

So, it becomes the manifestation of our self-preserving instinct that wherever we draw the line for personal leadership we simultaneously also draw the line with the kinds of relationships that can place the greatest demands on us to practice personal leadership.

And it is not that we do not want the bottom line honest truth challenging the most unstable or selfish parts of us. It is not that we just want to purposely get hit by the bus. It's just how little vulnerability that we want to give in exchange for being challenged.

This vulnerability would require us to present the selfish parts of our survival skills that we have purposely constructed to protect fear to now make the kinds of leadership decisions that will not allow us to remain selfish.

So, we look for alternative ways to secretly change the kinds of things that cannot be changed in secret in order to be able to control our healing. While at the same time controlling our safety nets and trust problems.

The only problem is that the more self-reliance you maintain the more self-deception you are prone to maintain right along with it. And some days the people who can help us the most in these situations are not the people we can use the pain or the injustice of our circumstances to manipulate their agreement or sympathy. They will not respond to sentimentalism as a way of permitting us to do what we want versus what we should.

CEO FACT:

We fall when we decide to fall. This is because all failure has nothing to do with who you are not being governed by. It only has to do with where you refuse to govern yourself.

Accountability is a decision we make to stay on course before it is a relationship we implement to help us accomplish that.

This is the reality about healthy relationships, even the ones we have for accountability purposes, is that no relationship will prevent failure.

Every major profession has codes and ethics that we are accountable to. Yes, the mere concept of accountability, if we implement it, can save us immense unnecessary damage.

But that is the lie of most people's understanding of failure; *"I fell because I did not have the proper accountability in my life."* Not an accurate perspective. Accountability on any level does not save us from where we are not functioning to save ourselves. Accountability does not save us from where we are not governing our own lives. That would be babysitting and sooner or later any of us can sneak out on the babysitter.

I personally have some wonderful peers in my life of whom I can discuss just about any piece of my dirty laundry with. But at the end of the day, I stay on track because of how I choose to govern myself on the track. If I don't, I will choose to self-destruct regardless of who is my support system. Staying on track is a decision to not be selfish before it's a decision to be accountable.

This is why *accountability is for people who want to stay on course at any cost. It does not make you stay on course.*

Staying on course in anything can cost us dearly some days. And it is where such a person does not like the cost that they will justify not having to pay it or at least will procrastinate when they have to.

Even when you have a whole cheering section screaming for you not to go off course, the reality for us is that we will only do what we have a vision to do—*either live to serve our anger or lust or live to serve our purpose.*

Yes, right relationships are great for our support and sobriety, not to mention dealing with our self-deception. But the bottom line of all success or failure is that where we draw the line for personal growth, we will also draw the line at where we will fight to govern against what can derail us. And we will draw this line regardless of who our inner circle is or is not.

CEO FACT:

Significant deterioration in anything always begins with the decision to influence the people below us, alienate the people above us, and network with the people just as wounded as us.

This is the last frontier of dealing with accountability issues. Coming to grips with the reality of where on any given day any of us can use a void of it to protect indifference as much as we can use the presence of it to protect success.

This is the issue. *None of us fail because we have no one to talk to. Failure usually broods in the midst of the kinds of things we do not want to talk about.* So, most people believe the lie that powerful people crash because *"it's so lonely at the top."* Not so. It's not more lonely, it's just more self-reliant.

The air is thinner, so it is easier to hallucinate and believe what is not real. It is also easier to believe the lie that *"I am too powerful or special to be understood."* Not so either.

People at the top are no different than people at the bottom when it comes to their problems. It's just that at the top your playground is bigger, and your fortresses are thicker.

So in times when it is easiest to fall prey to our own limited or at times, hurting and deceived perspectives, we will either connect with who is healthy, who is impressionable, or who is hurting too.

Healthy people will challenge our motives and integrity. These are the people above us in a particular area. Above meaning, people who have a degree of better character in an area that could be what preserves us on days we are ripe for storms because of where we lack character.

Whereas impressionable people, while being nice people, are still not the most honest ones. Sure they can see a lot of things, but their ability to be honest about what they see is too distorted by their motives for finding compatibility with our weaknesses instead of facilitating the change of them.

And the wounded . . . they do not even have to personally agree with us in order to justify our error. As a matter of fact, they are happy to place a positive spin on our blind spots as long as we agree to overlook theirs.

No, this is not to say that we need people who will just force help on us that we are not asking for. However, avoiding pitfalls is not only about what we can see clearly in our own paths. It is also about what the people around us can see and have nothing to lose by holding up the mirror up in front of us.

While impressionable and wounded people are nice for soothing our pain or just letting us vent, they are way too surface codependent and opportunistic in their own character to rattle us out of our most destructive modes.

CEO FACT:

Whatever you are, you will manifest when you are corrected.

On the brink of learning what could save you enormous amounts of future pain and loss, you will have to agree to hear certain things about yourself that you will not want to hear from people who have paid a price to be developed on a level that you have not paid yet.

One reason is because liberating change can only happen after you decide to stop personalizing what needs changing. Meaning, where you stop viewing core flaws in you through the shame of, *"You're a bad person"* and start seeing them as, *"Thank God now I see it so I can be a free person."*

So, my relationship with you cannot be considered legitimate until I do not have to be in your life so badly that I am forced to agree with and be silent about your deficiencies just to stay connected.

This is one reason why only a deceitful person desires networking without correction.

On a personal level, I realized a long time ago when it came to my learning process that *"not everyone who knew something that I needed to know, minded watching me struggle without it."* Meaning, everyone who could save me what my ignorances would cost me would not necessarily help me because they opened themselves up to me but rather because I opened myself up to them.

Thus, the real us, always surfaces during moments when we are wrong. One reason is because the measure of a person is only determined by what they are when they are wrong, not when they are right.

The word "correction" in of itself scares the average person because most people were taught to see correction from a perspective of being judged or abused more than taught. For many, correction was not a form of empowerment as it should have been, but a form of emotional neutering.

And for many of us, we were corrected wrong by people who were never corrected right themselves. So, they hurt us all in the name of helping us only because they were hurting too. That was not correction. That was the abuse of power, being used to compensate for another's unresolved abuse.

So, for abuse victims it is all too easy to be protective against deep levels of correction since the average correction was something you survived more than grew from. It meant exchanging identity for acceptance and safety.

However submitting to proper correction is never about losing yourself. It is about losing your blind spots.

All that bad correction does is leave us to be adult performers only because potential rejection is involved.

As adult performers we become adult competitors as well. However, this competitiveness is not out of the motive of winning along with helping others win. This is rather the motive of, *"I only win when I beat you."*

So, because of insecurity someone else has to lose in order for us to feel important. This concept works great in sports, but it is significantly destructive for relationships and real life.

However, with correction most people assume that it is hard to take. It's not. The hard part is letting go of the delusion that we could not be as inaccurate, incompetent, or inappropriate as we sometimes are.

Which is why we only react to what we are really guilty of. What we are not guilty of does not really phase us. Meaning, where someone says what they think we are, we cannot be devastated or be provoked to lash back, unless there is a measure of accuracy to what is said.

Remember: *A plan is not a plan or an important decision is not an important decision until you can open it up to the honest interrogation of someone else who can tell you something different about it than just what you were telling yourself.* Any decision that cannot survive the interrogation of unbiased feedback is just a problem waiting to happen.

And the only thing worse than fearing correction is not fearing how much of life that we waste when we are left to juggle the pressure of incompetence and presumption.

1.

You will never become any bigger than what you are if you are always the biggest person you relate to.

Rumor has it that a high profile author of a very successful motivational series of books whose name we can only refer to as Author A, phoned another best-selling author and motivational speaker, Tony Robbins. The apparent purpose was to discuss a comparison dilemma regarding their individual successes.

It wasn't that Author A thought his books were better, but rather that his proceeds lacked significantly in comparison to that of Tony Robbins who was making several times more per year give or take.

Author A's argument was that if his books were equal in overall content to Robbins, then why was his profit margin impact different?

As the story goes, Tony's response to Mark Author A was that Author A was the biggest person in his circle. Whereas, Tony, while making significantly more, still ran with other leaders who were at mega-millions and more.

Tony Robbins was making more because Tony Robbins was not the biggest guy in his circle. So, he was getting more out of his product and his potential because guys farther ahead of him were pulling it out of him.

You cannot be the biggest fish in your pond and then expect to become a bigger fish. Anyone in your life can only help you be what they are, bigger or smaller. And unfortunately, too many people consider this to be a successful goal when they can get to a place in life where they are the biggest dog on the porch.

The bottom line is that *no one can increase you until they are ahead of you in something.* So, you can run with those of your same size for encouragement and networking. You can run with those smaller than you to mentor them. But the moment you want to become bigger than what you are, you will have to connect with those who already are what you want to be. The danger of plateauing is that the only way to go is down.

➤ *You cannot only have a sentimental circle in your life and not an accountable one.*

Many people only have the former, not the latter. What the average person calls their advice circle is really just a circle for the affirmation of their own viewpoint and not a circle for change.

Your sentimental circle is often the people you are comfortable with. But your accountable circle is the people who can stretch you. *"Yes, but I have both in one circle."* Most would like to believe that, simply because they fear looking caught. However, the problem is when we think that we can be accountable to our sentimental circle.

That is kind of hard to do because sentimentalism involves so many personal attachments and personal accommodating, that direct honesty can get very watered down and lost.

Sentimental circles are comprised mostly of mutual history. Whereas accountable circles are comprised of mutual principle.

Both have benefit. It's just that sentimentalism will always err on the side of feeling safe, more than irritated enough to raise our game.

And what defines a shallow person? Someone who cannot separate loving you from loving the truth more.

People can only help you as effectively as the depth of reality about themselves that they function by.

Meaning, when someone makes it easier for you to connect with familiarity more than truth, they have just accelerated your setbacks.

Where is your behavior or personal integrity off course with where you need to be in this area?

How would the person you want to be handle this area differently?

Leadership is never greater than what it is easiest to be, good or bad, in the presence of your closest relationships.

21

CHOOSE YOUR RELATIONSHPS FOR WHERE YOU WANT TO BE.

Single people are big victims of this trap. They base commonality while on a date on getting to know where another person has come from.

Where did you grow up? Where did you go to school?

What planet did you live on before you came to earth? You know the drill.

The problem is that four courses of dinner, three glasses of wine, or six café mochas later, not to mention the extent of phone conversation or chat room chatter, they know very little about where the other person is headed.

The myth that where a person has come from says so much about them is not exactly accurate either. You can overlook or even agree over a lot of issues about a person's yesterday, but that does not mean that you want to be a part of their tomorrow.

The current divorce rate in America alone is not so staggering because you got to know a person's past. It is staggering because of where you were unaware or in denial about a person's future.

This is because of one truth; *you do not connect with a person. You connect with where a person is going, good or bad, and the kinds of lifestyle changes they are making to go there.*

I tell single people all of the time, *"You just don't marry a person. You marry their vision, or lack of one."* People are not determined by their past more than their future. The past is only an issue if their future is going to be spent re-creating more of their past.

So, when it comes to defining relationships *other people can only take you in the same direction they are going.* Meaning, it is the same people as us that make it possible for us to be us.

So, you do not just make relationships. You choose relationships based on where you want to go forward or backward. And since none of us are ever bigger than the relationships we keep, we cannot attract people out of weakness and then demand that they produce strength.

CEO FACT:

Who you permit around you will only sharpen or dull you to be just like them. And anything you must shrink to accommodate is never worth obtaining.

The standard you use to connect with people will be the same standard you will have to use to keep them.

So, you never just take on a relationship; you also take on everything they stand for and everyone else in their lives who stands for the same thing.

You will always know right people by how they increase the pace of your growth. You will know wrong people by how much they slow it down. So, when another person does not provoke the best in you, it is because they do not need you to be your best.

And it's your closest relationships that had better be nurturing the right things in you or they will sooner or later be feeding the wrong things in you.

This is because of one truth. *People can only energize the best in you, or the worst in you, depending on what energizes them.* So, right relationships are not the people who like you, and wrong relationships are not the people who hurt you. All relationships are determined by one thing—*what you want to be when you are around that person.*

For example, when I am around my ministerial heroes like Pastor Tommy Barnett even from a distance I want to immediately be a better leader and a bigger visionary.

When I watched the Mel Gibson directed movie, *The Passion of the Christ,* I left the theatre immediately wanting to be a better Christian. Sit in Donald Trump's presence for five minutes, and you would immediately want to be a better entrepreneur.

This is how you distinguish healthy relationships from unhealthy ones—*by what comes out of you when you are next to them.*

Many people across the country became acquainted with my public speaking and teaching through dozens of conferences that I shared with another nationally known leadership speaker who was at the time more prominent than I. Literally overnight I severed the relationship.

No, not because I got offended or caught this person in something. But people, still to this day, ask me repeatedly, *"What happened?"* My answer is simple, *"Being in the presence of this other leader made it way too easy for the worst things in me to thrive."*

When I am in the presence of dark people, then dark things come out of me. When I am in the presence of manipulative people, then rage comes out of me.

Any person will either energize the best in us, or the worst in us, depending on what energizes them.

So identifying wrong people is not that hard. They are simply the ones who make it easier for the worst parts of us to thrive the most.

And while we cannot get off by saying that wrong people make us self-destruct, since our own conduct is our own decision, still they assist us with how to self-destruct more effectively.

Besides, conquering dysfunction is already hard enough on its own without inviting people who celebrate dysfunction to connect with you and make yours worse.

CEO FACT:

People can only handle about you what they can handle about themselves. So, you wishing they could handle more will not fix it.

While it is true that you have to teach people how to treat you, you still cannot draw from a person what they are not deep enough to give you. So, you will never stop being unnecessarily derailed by the weaknesses of others until you are willing to accurately accept the kinds of things they may be incapable of giving you in their current state. And if you will not be so needy and so blinded when it comes to functioning out of your own unmet needs, then you will be able to look at anyone else's reactions and priorities, as well as, listen to their sense of reason in order to know clearly the limitations and duration, shallow or deep, that your connection with them will be.

It's like this: *all relationships are either what honesty or denial make them.* So, people do not have to necessarily be honest with you for you to be honest about them.

Jesus knew this about His own disciples. He not only knew when He would be betrayed and given over to savage authority by one of them, but He also knew how many of His remaining disciples possessed no capacity to support Him during His most trying time.

This is not a bad thing to know. *We don't often keep relationships healthy because of what other people know about themselves, but rather because of what we are willing to know about other people.* No, not about their secrets necessarily, but more about the patterns and tendencies they emanate.

Jesus knew His disciples could not process His ordeal because they could not process their own fears and identity problems at the time either.

The disciples could not give Jesus something that they could not give themselves. So, Jesus enjoyed His disciples on the levels He could and where He couldn't, He did not sabotage the relationship. *A person can only process about you what they can or cannot process about themselves.*

So, people will only hurt you after you thought they should be able to handle more, not to mention where you believed you could control them to do so.

So other people's flaws will not be what destroys their relationship with you. Your own refusal to determine the boundaries of where you can and cannot take their flaws will.

CEO FACT:

Your success will always come down to four kinds of people in your life.

1. Friends. No, not the television show.

Friends are not just people who accept your flaws. They are people who believe in your gifts more than your flaws and do not judge you while you are in the process of change. Besides, it is not friendship when we can link because of flaws; *it is mutilation.*

Friendship is primarily determined by two factors: what both parties have a desire to invest in each other, and what you are willing to work through together.

It is rarely about what you have in common.

Yes, chemistry plays a major role in any relationship, but how deep you will give to a relationship and how far you will protect the relationship from strife, not to mention your own selfishness and self-deception, plays a bigger role.

2. Allies. These are people who do not have to believe the same thing as you in order to want the same thing as you. Allies are people who have a piece of your goal that you do not have simply because you have a piece of theirs also.

So, you achieve together what you could not achieve alone. Besides, we lie to each other when we assume that we can describe unity in the light of being *"passivity all in the name of love."* It's not. Unity, rather, is when we are all big enough to see the gifts in each other that can bring us all to a mutual win-win end result.

3. Mentors. As a leader you can never assume that because you know your problems exist, you also know how deep they run.

The tragedy of insecure leaders is how they mentor themselves. So, the reason why God favors you with mentors or teachers is because while you are looking at the existence of your dysfunction, a mentor is looking at the eventuality of it.

And it is only those who can see something that you can't, that can help you reach somewhere you could not by yourself. So, mentors will offer access, not guarantees. And what you do with that access changes you, not them.

4. Enemies. Enemies facilitate conflict. Conflict facilitates change. And at no time can any of us rate our success by only those who like us.

So some days only those who do not need to be liked by you can provoke you to go the furthest.

At the end of the day we only grow two ways: *by the friends who work with our weaknesses and by the enemies who exploit them.*

CEO FACT:

Relationships have to agree on truth more than method. Which is why only in dictatorship is there no latitude for individual assignment.

The key to sustaining relationships is not found in cloning, but rather giving. *Anything based on cloning can only be maintained by superficiality.*

One reason we like to clone is to minimize potential disappointment. Since after all, it is always easiest to control what is just like us.

But cloning is denial and mutual deception, not relationship. And when denial is the common bond, then betrayal can only be the common fruit.

CEO FACT:

A relationship is only as good as what you are willing to protect about it.

When you take on any relationship you take on their wars. So, anyone is only as valuable to you as what you will or will not permit your enemies to say about them.

Which is why managing a relationship is as much about exposing strife as it is enlarging pleasure.

First of all, uncommon leaders do not spend their time attempting to adapt to who, and what, is not them. So, a person does not have to be bad in order to be wrong for you. And you will always know wrong relationships by how much misery you encounter from forcing them to be right.

Secondly, uncommon leaders do not need friends so badly that they accept opportunists instead.

The difference between friends and opportunists is friends will believe in who you are whereas opportunists will only believe in what you can give them.

An opportunist is simply a climber. They are someone who has the desire for gain without the desire for relationship. Climbers are those who can only support you in victory because supporting you in controversy would cost them too much.

Climbers only want the benefits of knowing you without the commitment of protecting you. So they will gossip to gain acceptance with you until it is more beneficial to gossip about you to gain acceptance with others.

Thirdly, uncommon leaders continually bless the people closest to them.

People see the government's lawsuit against the shrewd side of a Bill Gates to corner the software market while stonewalling the competition in the process. But his billions of dollars in donations to aid the research of cancer, aids, and to build schools often times goes off like a sidebar announcement on the too obscure to see it portion of the daily newspaper.

People see the fame of an Elvis. Or they see the exorbitant salaries of professional athletes. But uncommon acts of generosity are often said in passing more than recognition.

Atlanta Falcons running back, Warrick Dunn, buys homes for single moms. Some of Elvis's friends and relatives drove nice cars and lived in nice homes that they would have never been able to own without Elvis. *Uncommon leaders don't just have success. They share success.*

CEO FACT:

Your leadership will be impressive for your people knowledge but admired for your people skills.

An uncommon leader will work harder to maintain bridges than they will to burn them. One reason is because only uncommon leaders are never too successful to not have their pulse on the influence known as *"the personal touch."*

First of all, they take time to be personal. Any leader can appeal to the masses. Only uncommon leaders know how to appeal to an individual.

They don't just send cards, gifts, et cetera, they send cards and gifts with a personal handwritten sentence or remark and signature. *One relational sentence will always go farther than several nonrelational paragraphs.*

So, an uncommon leader will even take time to find out things you like so that they can respect your taste more than expect you to have theirs.

Secondly, they look you in the eye when they are talking to you. Not just because you matter, but mostly because they do not demand respect; *they sow it.* They give what they expect others to give to them.

Thirdly, they work hard to know your name.

Not just because they are good at being diplomatic but mostly because they relate to where they are at that moment and not where they wished they were.

Fourthly, they are approachable. When someone cannot touch you, they can sooner or later figure out a way to not need you.

Besides, people have enough problems without needing to worry about being impressed by your importance as another one.

Fifthly, they are gracious. Oscar winning actor, Sir Anthony Hopkins, was sitting in a Southern California deli ordering a hamburger when the waiter recognized who he was. The waiter began impersonating the actor's famed movie character, Hannibal Lector.

Sir Anthony graciously smiled and upon leaving, left the waiter a hundred dollar tip and the number to a local acting school. *Even in the midst of undesirable circumstances or undesirable people, an uncommon leader demands class of themselves first, regardless of who does not have it around them.*

They do not make the valet feel like a peon nor do they remind the waiter who brought them an undercooked steak that they will never be anything else better than a waiter.

1.

You must ask every relationship, "Who are you, and why are you connected to me?"

1. What comes out of you when you are around them? The common link of any relationship decides the common fruit that is multiplied, good or bad.

2. Did your weaknesses attract them or did your strengths? People of lesser character will require your character to compensate.

3. Do they remind you of the person you do not want to be anymore or the person you are supposed to be now? You will only answer this when you can assess the kinds of things that come out of you when you are around them.

Some days it takes yesterday people leaving your life just to help you get out of yesterday. Some days it takes who you can no longer hang around with to show you the level you are no longer on as a person.

4. Do they reach for you when they do not need anything? People only protect what they build with you, not what they use you to build.

5. Are they a network, or are they a friend? People who only want to network with you can only handle your ideas. They cannot handle your flaws or your secrets. So, don't confuse them with friends.

Friends stay with you because of you. Networkers only stay with you because of a destination they need to reach because of you.

6. How much do you have to slow down in your life just to be in theirs? How much can't you share, discuss, or solicit feedback from them concerning your personal vision for success? How transparently can't you discuss you're most sensitive challenges? Someone who cannot celebrate your progress, cannot contribute to your progress.

So it's when you discuss your changes with an identity crisis person that you are really expecting someone who hates their life to actually love your greatness.

Remember. Your confidence will never be mentored by the inferior.

7. Who have they increased? It's kind of presumptuous to assume that you are going to be a better person for having someone in your life if no one else has.

Often times you will never know what a person will bring to your life until you can honestly assess what they have brought to someone else's.

And since someone without the drive to improve themselves will also be without the capacity to improve you, you will have to know people by what they add or take away and not by longevity.

2.

You will never succeed with people you are trying to rescue.

Rescue their perception of you. Rescue their unwillingness to live by a code of conduct that you wished they had. Rescue them from rejecting you.

We only rescue people because of what is wrong with us, not what is wrong with them. Marriages do this. It's the, *"You're the one for me, now let me change you to not disappoint me"* syndrome.

However, the problem where indifferent and abusive people are concerned is they are not going to let you fix them more than they will just allow you to try.

This is because your attempt at fixing them takes the attention off of their own conviction to fix themselves. So, then you cry hurt because they are not changed while they get a reprieve from having to change because of your codependent effort.

Remember. Who you decide to be has nothing to do with who other people are. So, what a person is, is what you will get until the day they are convicted to be anything better.

So if you are committed to your own growth, then your growth will either be the great equalizer that convicts change in the people who want to be different or places distance between you and the people who don't care.

Either way, you will only rescue people who are not growing, because you aren't growing either.

3.

Make a list of some people you may need to send some apologies to.

Apologies disarm pride. Pride is blinding. Many days the only reason we do not see the negative effects that we may have on other people is because we are afraid too. Besides, you must take advantage of every opportunity you have to allow humility to relieve the pressure of selfish behavior brought on by fear.

Where is your behavior or personal integrity off course with where you need to be in this area?

How would the person you want to be handle this area differently?

Leadership is only as commanding as your ability to play hurt, not take warfare personally and not faint at the sight of blood.

22

YOUR SUCCESS WILL ONLY BE AS CREDIBLE AS YOUR ABILITY TO REMAIN PRODUCTIVE DURING TOUGH TIMES.

Success is not what we obtain because nothing breaks down. It is what we obtain from staying productive in spite of what has broken.

With conquering the sometimes stressed out, bewildered, and unpredictable dynamics of adversity one truth is magnificent in its importance of whether you master times of adversity or they master you; *we cannot always control why we are in some battles. We can only control how we come out of them.* And we can only control how we come out of a battle by what we choose to turn the battle into while we are still in it.

Meaning, many people never play beyond their injuries because their limited sense of self-sobriety left them no room to be injured. So, the fact that they could even get hurt consumes them far too much to stay in the game long enough to achieve something bigger than their wounds.

Conflict will always surround the birth of significant change. So, success is never success because you don't walk with a limp. It is refusing to give attention to the limp.

Enemies are only the proof you have potential bigger than your problems. So, you will only take your enemies personal when you are not taking your potential personal enough.

This is also where you will battle with depression from the anger of what you resent that hasn't changed on its own before you would have to step up and change it.

CEO FACT:

In any situation there is only wisdom. Everything else is just emotion.

Some days we never truly know the magnitude of what needs changing in or around us until we decide to move to a new level with it and can't.

So in every conflict you must find the wisdom of the conflict regardless of where the wisdom may not agree with your perspective of what the conflict is.

You see, often times it is too easy to only look for wisdom that agrees with how you want to feel about your situation. And the secret to moving forward in anything is always found in the realm of what is bigger than just what we felt.

This is one reason why the average person does not understand closure to painful issues or seasons of life. *Closure is not you out-grieving pain; rather, it is you outgrowing pain.* So, when it comes to yesterday, you will never place closure to anything until you are using the new you to do it.

Closure is when something that could only be connected to the old you can now be released because of the new you. This is also why forgiveness in anything is only possible when we are the ones different and not when our enemies are.

CEO FACT:

Your response to false accusation will determine how far off course your enemy can get you.

Remaining productive during tough times simply comes down to how tough you agree to be with the hooks that can lure you into turning what any battle is . . . into multiple streams of what the battle is not supposed to be.

These hooks will only succeed when they can make your adversity about you instead of the next levels of purpose and prosperity that are awaiting you.

One of the costliest hooks is the place where we will agree to defend our tough times against the judgments and criticisms from people who are not only afraid to relate to our pain, but are also indifferent towards helping us resolve it.

This is the basis of false accusation. Or what some call slander or gossip. False accusation or gossip can be a lot of things. But one thing that it is more than anything—*it is rarely about you.*

Accusation, or all unnecessary chatter about you for that matter, is usually a smokescreen for what your accuser is guilty of themselves. Accusation is also the indicator of how empty your accusers are within themselves. Of course, it is just easier to discuss you. So, false accusation is about others who see the ability to use something about you as their way of protecting something about themselves.

Accusation does not have anything to do with you even being guilty of the crime. It has to do with how badly devious and insecure people need to manage illusion more than fact.

So accusers are never people grieved over you. They are people afraid of themselves. They are addicted to the division of something. They are not people into truth either. They are people on the run. And you can always tell what they are running from by what they attack in you.

It is just easiest to know where your accusers are guilty themselves, because there is not the spirit of grace or compassion, only the spirit of judgment. *And judgmentalism is really just the anger of guilt masked in the cloak of hypocrisy.*

So you want to study times of false accusation or gossip for one primary reason. Accusation does not just reveal who would share lies or even secrets about you. It also reveals who would listen to them and who would believe it.

It's like this: *Emotional people will guard you when they like you. Character people will guard you when they don't.* So, anyone who would entertain accusation against you is not in your life to build anything with you.

There you have it.

Accusation or slander will not make sense to you. So you cannot respond to it sensibly. Just stay focused on what you are building more than what you are defending. Build something with your life so great that anyone with less integrity looks foolish to criticize it.

Remember: *Accusers are not people without potential, they are people without vision. And it will only be people with distorted vision who will attempt to kill yours.*

CEO FACT:

How you help others in their adversities will only come back as a harvest of how others will help you.

Tenderheartedness is not what you develop after you forgive. It is what you develop after you realize how far others have had to go to forgive you.

It's like this: *Generations are never prospered because its leaders do not lose their way, but rather because its leaders do not lose their dream.* So, often times when you stand by someone in their failure, you are not just standing by them because you like them or feel sorry for them. You are standing by what it will mean to the future of others who will benefit if such a person is not destroyed.

Always remember this: *When you reach for the underdog you always force the reality of false friendships to emerge.* In other words, some days you have to help someone else in crisis just to expose the people around you who would never help you in crisis.

1.

Don't breathe life into anything that is not the big picture of the circumstance.

The big picture of any situation in front of you is the only chance you have at staying off of what has been referred to in other portions of this book as being *the low road.*

The low road of any conflict is the part where the conflict is exploited by the drama of the conflict instead of the resolve of the conflict. And when you refuse to take the bait of the low road, then your greatest stability is established.

➤ *Keep conflict about the issue of what it really is. It is about your change. It is not about your enemy.*

➤ *Focus on something better that you want as a result of the conflict. Do not focus on the fact that you are hurt.*

We make changes because of a level of fulfillment we refuse to live without. We avoid changes because of a level of fulfillment we have convinced ourselves we can live without.

➤ *You have to solve the big picture in anything or you will just be managing the chaos of it.* Change in anything begins with today. If you are going to change something, then you cannot become so enchanted with how it got messed up.

2.

Keep what is the truth about your purpose as the criteria for responding to any situation.

Meaning, learn to answer all conflict based on what you are called to become, instead of just based on what you are going through or how you feel.

In her last appearance at the Crystal Cathedral in Southern California, years before her eventual death, civil rights widow, Coretta Scott King, stated that her only refuge for coping with the enormous pain of losing her husband, Dr. Martin Luther King Jr., prematurely to an assassin's bullet, was that she knew her purpose in life was to stand by the side of her great man for as long or short as he would be on the earth. When Dr. King Jr. died early in his mission, she could still say that she had fulfilled her purpose. She used her purpose in life as the filter for her pain. This is also why many people live so enraged and ultimately so self-defeating; they keep trying to explain injustice in order to define life rather than explaining life by defining purpose.

Dr. Phil calls them "sound bites." Meaning, definitive statements you develop that states who you are and where you are going. These become the compasses of sorts to keep you on track through stormy weather.

➤ *Train your responses to be from a position of moving forward.* Moving forward is not about not being guilty in whole or in part of the crime. It is about not being paralyzed by it. Any response that keeps you moving forward will never keep you angry or broken down. Anger is just the fruit of managing the things that you have permitted to stop you.

3.

Respect is not what you earn by never falling down, but rather how you get back up.

Recoveries are not for the pretty, but for the relentless. So it is all too easy to fall underneath a battle because of the public's perception of your battle you are trying to protect the most during your battle.

And while it is good to build a right reputation through acts of integrity and consistency, still when all is said and done, *if you lose your reputation you've lost little. If you lose your edge you've lost everything.*

4.

Never seek help in getting up from those still lying down.

Those who cannot be honest about their pain will never be able to prescribe your cure. Restoration will never be about the sin you do time for. It is about the character deficiencies you make changes in.

So, God's schedule for your turnaround will never seem logical to those who weren't trying to get you back in the game.

Besides, truth tainted with pain is not truth. It is a hang-up. So, you will never find compassion from people who give you hypocrisy.

Where is your behavior or personal integrity off course with where you need to be in this area?

How would the person you want to be handle this area differently?

Leadership is never determined by not failing more than not quitting.

23

ANYONE CAN FIGHT WHEN THEY HAVE INSPIRATION. ONLY CHAMPIONS CAN FIGHT WHEN THEY DON'T.

It is always mediocre people that want increase without inconvenience. And you will only initiate increase the moment you are willing to pay more for what you want than you had to pay for what you have.

It is encountering conflict that is where our purpose is refined. But growing bigger than conflict is where our purpose is revealed. Which is why *your plans can change, but your fight cannot.*

Which also means recoveries are not for the pretty, but for the relentless. So, getting back up in anything is a fight, more than a beauty contest.

Your fight is the only thing that keeps taking you back to the drawing board until the answers you need emerges.

Yes, all adversity interrupts. But most interruptions only hurt as bad as where we lack resolve towards our purpose, rather than our plans.

Meaning, fallen people stay sidelined because their plans were as devastated as their concept of falling down was. So, the rest of them just became devastated too.

CEO FACT:

Your ability to win in anything will come down to your ability to take a punch.

The punch is only what makes you fall down. It is never what makes you stay down.

So, it is not that the average person cannot take a hit. It's just that most people assume they would never be hit as hard or as often as they were, or in some cases even hit at all.

CEOs who assume that their corporations would never be investigated or divided. Parents who assume little Susie would never come home on birth control, or little Johnny would never come home high.

The average person does not live with an accurate assessment of conflict or failure.

No, you do not need to stand in the punching line as a way to show your toughness. But where you have a sober sense of taking a punch, then while any punch can produce pain and blood and even knock you down, still where it was allowed to be a wake-up call rather than the end of the world, then it will only just be what it is; *a punch.*

And you will never survive a punch where you lack the vision for what is on the other side of getting hit.

Just the sheer cold slap we sting with upon encountering conflict or making mistakes, hurts us more than we can explain some days. And it is not that having some great personal vision will somehow magically take away our all of our pain. But what it will do is keep us moving towards a right destination greater than our pain, even on the days when we are still hurting.

The average person only stays down after taking a punch because they want to blame the punch rather than their own lack of resolve. So you will only lack the resolve for getting up where you lack the esteem to see yourself better than the punch. It is your self-respect that drives you to reach for something bigger than the punch. Without self-respect all you are is a martyr for pain.

And with any punch, it is only as devastating as how quickly we refuse to get up.

This would explain why society is filled with people who were hit years ago, but are still lying on the mat in their mentality and their coping skills today.

This is what all people do when they have never grown beyond their distorted reality of being hit; *they spend the rest of their lives dressing the bruise with external success, rather than growing thicker skin than the bruise and growing their boundaries to stop absorbing the same repetitive hits.*

Which becomes the issue in the beginning of this point—*the punch is only what makes you fall down. It is never what makes you stay down!*

CEO FACT:

Take responsibility that all loss begins and ends with you.

- *Your failure is not your employee's fault. You hired them.*
- *Your failure is not your spouse's fault. You married them.*
- *Your failure is not a Judas' fault. You trusted them.*
- *Your failure is not even your fault. It is the fault of the person you have been that you are now being given the chance to change. Other people may have helped your fall, but your present standard decided it.*

Other circumstances may have contributed to your pain but somewhere either your decisions or your blind spots positioned you in the line of fire.

Okay. You thought that recovery was the product of compassion more than responsibility. Not really.

You will blow it. All risk takers do. Restructure your plan, your information, or your approach and move on. Streamline your wisdom, rather than your ego.

Remember: *We fall down because of what we lack, but we get back up because of what we learn.* So, the only thing worse than the strain of conflict is the indifference towards understanding.

And you will never change when unfortunate circumstances or unprincipled people change. You change when your personal standard changes.

1.

Stay out of the whys.

Why did someone who was supposed to love you right, or never leave you, not love you right and not protect you better?

Why are you the one having to deal with this or that crisis at this point in your life?

Whys only fuel rage that comes from feeling helpless to the parts of a problem that you have no control to fix. While you then use speculation to create additional parts of the problem that don't exist, which only produces more rage.

There is only rage in why, because in the why we are forced to make sense of insanity and injustice. And the deepest anger any of us will ever be tempted to fall into will be the anger from issues that we did not ask for, but we still have to be the ones to grow past.

➤ *Stay out of the stories.* People have stories when they don't have plans. Meaning, stories about yesterday because they have no ideas for where they want to be tomorrow.

Memories regardless of good ones or bad ones are only what connect you to what you cannot fix, change, or bring back.

This is why *success is not the ability to change memories, but rather the ability to change direction in spite of the memories.*

Remember: *you cannot disperse the past if you rehearse the past.*

➤ *Watch what you come out swinging with.* Moving on in anything is not about being pain free, but rather about not being pain dependent. This anger is not over taking a hit, more than it is over where our world stopped at the place where we did.

So, we will come out swinging against the world attempting to reverse it. The problem is usually all of the destructive weapons that our anger will come out swinging with that will be incapable of facilitating any kind of healthy comeback.

2.

Look at your responses.

Nothing derailing ever leaves your life until you stop handling it the same way. The same bad approaches just keep fueling the same bad repetitive patterns.

Obstacles don't move; you move around obstacles. Obstacles don't change. You change, and then you leave the obstacle. So, what you see determines how you respond. Selective sight never sees accurate solutions.

➤ *Look at where you blame obstacles.* Blame only helps you coexist with what you resent having to change. It also justifies the indifference towards personal responsibility.

➤ *Look at where you process obstacles through codependence.* Codependence simply means that you are waiting for the obstacle to change before you can move on. While at the same time hoping that the obstacle will apologize to you for getting in your way.

Codependence is also when you choose to be a victim of an obstacle. The problem is that you will victimize others from where you are living like a victim.

➤ *Look at where you avoid unbiased counsel and accountability in how to remove an obstacle.*

Disarming obstacles is not about just seeing the obstacle; it is about seeing who you are inside of the obstacle.

So the greatest counsel to your obstacles will be the counsel that does not always agree with why you believe your obstacle is an obstacle.

3.

Manage your most productive state and your most fulfilling lifestyle.

Most people do not have a fulfilling weekly lifestyle that they manage. They have one or two weeks of vacation per year that they live for. Managing you is how you live your life by commitment on days when there is no inspiration.

➤ *What are the things daily and weekly that you need to be the most productive you?*

Billionaire, Donald Trump eats the same hamburger at the same restaurant multiple times a week in New York.

Actress, Jennifer Lopez is at the gym by 5 AM most days.

King David in the Bible would wake up before sunrise to pray. Ben Franklin would wake up at 4 AM every day and do all of his work by noon to have the rest of the day to himself.

➤ *What are the things that you have to have every week to be the most alert and fulfilled you?*

What are the movies or television programs that you have to see? What are the exercise routines that you have to engage in? What are the top meals or top two or three restaurants that you have to eat at? Anything that can refresh you can retool you.

➤ *What are the places that you have to frequent that clear your mind?* If you don't have time to refresh your mind, you will not have time to refine your plan.

➤ *Who are the friends that you have to see?*

➤ *What are the specific outfits that you have to wear?* Fashion changes your outlook, not other people's. What is the color or fit of the most productive you?

➤ *What time do you need to wake up in order to feel like you are getting a jump on all of your priorities?*

➤ *List your phone time.* When you return calls, or connect with friends, associates, et cetera.

➤ *Effective people also manage exits as much as entries.* Meaning, they place conclusions to everything. Conclusions, not beginnings, are how we manage time.

➤ *List the things that are important, but are flexible.* Meaning, you can do them at several different spots of the week.

➤ *Break up your priorities into windows of achievable stages.* You not only can eat one elephant a bite at a time, but you might be surprised that you could actually eat two or three.

Where is your behavior or personal integrity off course with where you need to be in this area?

How would the person you want to be handle this area differently?

Leadership is recognized by what we speak into others. But it is developed by what others speak into us.

24

NEVER SUBMIT YOUR PLANS TO THE COUNSEL OF ANYONE WHO DOES NOT OWN A HEAD.

A shepherd boy gets up to make his acceptance speech as the new captain of King Saul's army.

He takes the podium amidst the jeers of everyone older than him demanding to know why he was the nobody who had earned the right to be their new leader.

Without words of self-defense or sterile campaign promises he reaches down into his waist sack and takes out the head of a nine foot, nine inch giant named Goliath and places it up on the podium. Immediately the jeers and comments silence.

Why? David, the former shepherd boy, was the only one in the whole place who owned what none of the rest of them did—*an enemy's head.* The rest of them were too busy hiding from Goliath. David was too busy killing him (see 1 Samuel 17).

This is pivotal when it comes to the reality of who has the capacity to sharpen you and who does not. *David did not have the calling for leadership, he had the proof of leadership!* Everybody has the calling. Just not everybody wants to kill the kind of giants it takes to lead.

This is also one reason why so many people quit when facing their own giants; *who they are listening to in the midst of their battles.*

CEO FACT:

The level of life that you want to live on will decide the people you will listen to that can get your there.

The rewards of leadership are often found in who is listening to us. But the depth of leadership or lack of it is found in who we are listening to. *Right teachers are not those who help you cope with today, they help you leave it. And one right teacher can help you leave a season of life as fast as one wrong blind spot can help you stay.*

So, you cannot make healed decisions in the midst of broken people, and you cannot take healthy steps in the midst of selfish counsel.

Which would also explain why *it requires someone to see what you cannot see in order to help you arrive at a level you could not reach by yourself.* And none of us ever just decide our level of learning. *We decide our level of growth, and our level of growth decides our level of learning.*

So, where you cut off your desire for improvement, you will also cut off the kinds of relationships that can improve you. This is also where we live by the myth that *"truth hurts."* Not so. Truth docs not hurt. Lying to ourselves does.

CEO FACT:

Wise teachers will never teach you on your level or on your terms. Those who teach you on your terms can only teach you how to repeat your same struggles.

You will know a right teacher several ways.

They will not chase you.

They will not pursue you. They will give you access to pursue them.

They will not fight for you. They will teach you how to fight for yourself.

They will debate with your blind spots, but they will not defend themselves against them.

They won't request accountability; *they will demand it.* Their life does not change if you do not embrace what they know; *yours does.*

This is usually where we bristle as learners over the price of accountability. Accountability is not ownership. It is giving someone your honesty in exchange for their insight.

Accountability requires your vulnerability. It does not require you signing over your independence.

Which is one way you will know a great truth has been imparted into you by the fruit of interdependence, not codependence.

Meaning our indifference towards accountability is never because we fear being hurt. It is because we fear the games that we use to cover inadequacy actually exposing us as more undone than we want to appear.

And since bad teachers will cultivate bad behavior whereas right teachers will confront it, part of changing your defects is changing the relationships that have taught you that it is okay to be defective. So we will either relate to two kinds of people in the midst of any battle—*those who win battles* or *those who cover up for why they have even been in any*.

This is also when you change your teachers then you change your playing field. June Jones coaching the Atlanta Falcons at the time did not know what to do with a little known rookie quarterback named Brett Favre. Mike Sherman in Green Bay did. Brett Favre went on to win three most valuable player awards plus a Super Bowl championship. People who cannot recognize the champion in you will never pull the best out of you to be one.

CEO FACT:

Your learning will never surpass the level of questions you ask.

Two secrets of learning are: *you get what you sow for, and you get what you ask for.*

Solomon, while in the presence of God Himself, did not make small talk or clam up. He did not ask God, *"So what is it like to be you?"* Or *"What's your favorite planet?"* He asked God for wisdom. He became the smartest and richest man to ever live because of the one thing he asked for while with the Creator of all wisdom. *In the presence of those who can change your world, they will not talk for conversation more than solutions.*

Shallow people ask shallow questions. And personal progress is never about the ability to cure your ignorances while being able to look good in the process.

So, the dilemma of questions: the problem with either not knowing what to ask or being too afraid of what you may have to change if you do. So you protect blind spots because you would rather protect fear or pride.

And the big question . . . *"What are the best questions?"*

Ask questions for instruction, not affirmation. Anyone can compliment you, but not everyone can increase you. Mentors are there to challenge your insecurity, not accept it.

Goals must survive the scrutiny of wise counsel or they are just problems waiting to happen.

Ask questions for where you want to be. Anyone can discuss where you are. But not everyone can discuss how to go anyplace greater.

Mentors do not want to discuss much of how you got to this point. They discuss where you are going past this point.

Ask, "What do you see that I am not seeing?" What you gain through your strengths you will lose through your blind spots.

Ask embarrassing questions. No question is a dumb question to a teacher. So, you will only fear succeeding as long as you fear appearing undone.

The wisest mentors already know you are more screwed up than you think. Mentors already know you have problems, which would explain how you found them. Right mentors aren't shocked by your mess. But they will become very impatient with your denial or your arrogance about your mess.

1.

Ask yourself, "Do the people I am listening to the closest, have the fruit of strength in the areas where I need to grow?"

Anyone you listen to can only help you be just like who they are in their current state. So, you cannot win with what has not produced a victory for someone else.

When someone else speaks into your life who is not emanating the kind of strength that you need in your life, then you actually allow them to make your weaknesses worse. Which means *you want people who have the fruit of victory, not the illusion of victory.* Meaning, you want proven people with the victories of leadership more than the title of leadership.

Besides, it is only unproven teachers who will just expect you to follow what they would never follow themselves in the same situations.

➤ *Only discuss your most fragile parts with people ahead of you.* People ahead of you can pull. You cannot be pushed to victory . . . only pulled. People ahead of you will not judge you. They are not easily shocked.

2.

Never discuss problems with those incapable of solving them.

Indiscreet people will repeat out of vulnerability what you tell them out of vulnerability. So when you discuss a traitor with a traitor, they will need to be accepted by both sides. Which is how you will spot a betrayer—by how much more they achieve with your secrets than with your wisdom.

Where is your behavior or personal integrity off course with where you need to be in this area?

How would the person you want to be handle this area differently?

Leadership is never about the ability to lead the masses. It is about the ability to separate the masses from who will pay to be a part of the solution versus who will pay to stay a part of the problem.

25

YOUR LIFE WILL BE THE CLASSROOM FOR THE NEXT GENERATION.

Your successes are never the key to someone else's success, *your failures are.* This is because leaders cannot teach from their success, *only their mistakes.*

This is also why true mentoring of others does not place you on a pedestal. It actually knocks you off of one given how humble you become because of how transparent you have to be.

That is what mentoring is: *Teaching other people from what you are, not what you think they should be. Teaching without using yourself as your own best example is not teaching. It is actually hypocrisy mixed with dictatorship.*

So, now that you are effectively off of your pedestal . . . the real reason for why God allows any of us to go through certain experiences, that at times we are the most certain nothing good can come of, is because someone else's entire future rides on something painful you were willing to overcome. Otherwise said, *God gives every leader a past so they can give someone else a future.*

You thought God allowed you to survive something painful just because He thought you were special. Actually you survived because He thought other people He would connect you to were just as special.

So, this becomes the parts of you that you are willing to fix that ultimately becomes the only proof of how much you care in the success of future generations after you. Meaning, other people are not a success because of what they can do for you, but what they can do as the result of you.

So it is only what you put into a person that says everything about what you believe about them.

CEO FACT:

You are unqualified for leadership unless you are prepared to take others as far as you and in less time by using the insight from your own past failures to do it.

The only thing worse than failing is not helping others succeed. So, while what a leader prepares to succeed beyond them is the proof of vision, what a leader does not build to succeed beyond them is only the proof of abuse.

One could dismiss this truth by equating it only to a president or CEO of a mega organization. However, there are a lot of deficient parts of society ailing in present day because a man or woman never taught their son or daughter to be a better husband/wife or parent then they were and with less time sacrificed.

Leadership does not mean that you kill other people's giants for them. It means that you teach them how to conquer for themselves. It's just that on the flip side of this, any leader without any passion to help others become more, will also be without any guilt in watching them become less.

So it's when your passion is not for the increase of someone else that you will mostly impart to them everything that has decreased you.

And what makes an uncommon leader is not how few flaws they possess, but rather how few lives they will intentionally deteriorate due to defending those flaws.

It's when you defend your limitations that you are really defending what is broken in you. And the moment you accept anything broken, you are in line to believe deception. So, the next generation cannot help but either repeat your integrity or your dysfunction depending on which one you practiced more of.

Yes, you can only teach others from the changes you've made and not the changes you intend to make.

CEO FACT:

Deliverers are always victims first.

Pain does not give you identity. Growing past pain does. So, the authority to lead others to something good can only come from your willingness to lead yourself past something bad. You can only lead out of what has provoked depth and not what has provoked hatred.

It is your life assignment that reveals your warfare. Warfare meaning, the specific problems that you have been gifted to solve that have evolved through the specific types of obstacles you have had to overcome in order to know how to solve them.

That is one thing we cannot do—*study how to solve uncommon problems.* You can only make uncommon decisions in the midst of your own most undesirable situations, and then teach other people how to do to same thing.

Yes, God could have probably spared you from experiencing some of the problems that you did. But He could have also left you illiterate and undeveloped.

CEO FACT:

Any leader can easily develop the largest following anytime there is the enchantment of surface wisdom without the effectiveness of deep correction.

In Bible terms we could call this the *"Gideon Principle."* Meaning, the King, who had an army of thirty-two thousand, who was facing an army of over one hundred thousand only to hear God tell him, *"Scale down your army."*

Gideon, of course, asks what we all would, "W*hy?*" God replies back, *"You've got too many."*

No, it does not make sense in the numbers side of things. But that is one of the greatest leadership pitfalls: the desire to appeal to too much of the mass at the risk of not knowing just how much of the mass is or is not with you. Of course, until the battle forces you to find out the hard way. And in understanding the significant frailties of leadership, *the greatest perversion of truth is when we want growth without change.*

Which makes it way too easy if you are the leader not to know the answer to this. Only because of how easy it is to be blinded by the hope that everyone is what you believe they could be.

God was not telling Gideon that he had too many men. He was telling Gideon that *"you have too many men not in a position to fight."* Ironically, Gideon scaled down at God's command and won.

How? He watched them drink. No, not at the local pub. God told him to take all of his men down to the brook and watch how they drank.

Why? Because the ones that can help you facilitate victory will drink differently than the ones that can only facilitate defeat.

People in your circle, whether family or friends, that can facilitate the best in you will always function by a different code than those who can only facilitate the worst. The eagles always fly differently than the ducks. Get it?

Three hundred of Gideon's men drank differently than the other 31,700.

And as a leader, *most days you will never see the most productive people around you until it is time to defend something.*

Gideon had thirty-two thousand men who liked being in the group, but he only had three hundred who liked stepping up for the war. *People just have to like you to be connected to you. But they have to like leadership in order to produce victory with you.*

CEO FACT:

In order to effectively develop anyone wanting to learn from you, you will have to risk losing them in the process.

The standard you use to win people will also be the same standard you will have to maintain to keep them.

Welcome to the Gideon principle part two. The part about winning battles that is a heart issue before it is a competence one. Meaning, the reality that it is in the heart that those around you decide how much of a price they will or will not pay to win the gold.

Gideon did not teach his eventual three hundred how to drink right. It's like CEOs who ask me to come in and teach lectures on increasing team loyalty. I tell them I can't. You can't teach loyalty. You can only teach character and loyalty comes from character. *People give you what is in them, good or bad, and they give to you out of the excellence they are or are not willing to develop.*

As much as we would like to make leadership about the ability to, as in Gideon's position, teach people how to lead like we want, people are only going to lead with what is really in them. So while the thirty-two thousand can give you skill, the three hundred can give you heart. And you will never win a battle with anyone who cannot give you sacrifice above good intention. Whether in a marriage or a football team.

But remember: People will only leave your life for two reasons. *They could not go any further, or they did not want to.* So, when a person does not change by being in your life, then that is the proof they did not come into your life to change.

So, while what you will not invest into a person says what you did not want them to become, what another person does not permit you to invest in them says what they did not want to become.

And it's only through knowledge that you can decrease another's dependence on you. So, the moment you are willing to fight harder for another person's success than they are willing to fight to succeed, then all you will end up with is hirelings. *Hirelings are just passionless servers without integrity.*

And one thing about an uncommon leader is they will never spend valuable time attempting to improve those who have no passion for improving themselves.

Company CEOs are not just the only ones prone to having hirelings. People everywhere you go have hireling friends, hireling supporters, even hireling relatives. Heck, I've met people who have hireling spouses. Hirelings can be found in any environment simply because of the agenda you need them for.

Which is also why *your vision will never be diverse enough to accommodate the indifferent, strong enough to develop the unteachable, and big enough to hide the rebellious.*

1.

Never open a door for anyone not trying to kick it down.

Leadership is not simply the ability to teach truth; rather, it is the ability to only teach those hungry for the truth.

2.

Never teach a cheap or lazy person.

People who never pay for solutions never pay to apply solutions either. Remember the definition of a parasite from chapter ten? *They are people who want for free what it has cost someone else everything to obtain.*

No, this is not an issue of refusing to help those in a bad spot or who don't know any better. This is an issue that what any person wants, they go after. You teaching out of your sympathy more than their effort will only lead to you carrying them more than they are walking.

3.

You can only teach from the flaws that you are not hiding and conflict you are not personalizing.

It is only abusive to expect others to be more honest with you then you are about you.

As a leader, most people wanting your help will not enter your life because they have problems. They will enter because they are hoping you don't have the same ones.

So, the average person entering your life in need of help will not expect you to see the dysfunctional parts of you more clearly than they assume they can see about you.

It's like this. People can only use against you what you are hiding. So, when you bring your own imperfections from a place of being hidden to being *"out of the box," (as my psychologist friend, Violet Arnold, would teach)* people are forced to then take their own issues seriously. As opposed to just being able to use their disappointment with your obvious flaws as the excuse not to. It's when you can discuss you better than anyone else can discuss you that you disarm yourself of the pressure from juggling other people's blame, criticism, and their desire to use your darkness to hide their own.

Oh, and the taking our conflicts personal part, it is when you personalize conflict that you limit your ability to impart wisdom from it. What you impart more is animosity. Then you teach other people how to take on the identity of your pain rather than the identity of your growth.

Where is your behavior or personal integrity off course with where you need to be in this area?

____

____

____

____

____

____

____

How would the person you want to be handle this area differently?

____

____

____

____

____

____

____

Leadership never fails because of the mistakes you make more than the mistakes you manage.

26

MAKING ROOM FOR WHAT YOU WANT.

The reality of this chapter has perhaps been the greatest turning point of my personal life.

I made a statement in the foreword section of this book that *you can change any situation in your life by changing who you are in that situation.* This was how I got it. I literally put an end to years of anxiety, stress, low self-respect, a wounded orphaned heart, and all of the manipulation, excessiveness, and out of control anger I was using to medicate it. *I changed what I was managing.*

More realistically, I began the process to stop managing.

I have to emphasize the word *"process"* because most of what we manage that is unhealthy and deficient becomes trained behavior. So, the process to change anything negative that we manage is to untrain why we manage it. *Anything learned can be unlearned.*

No, this wasn't some magical day where angels entered my bedroom and solved all my problems. Yes, I kept managing my work, my finances, my duties to my children, my business issues, and my responsibilities as a leader. But those issues were not what were contributing to my completely angry and unfulfilled state. They were only being clouded by everything that was.

All of us move in the direction of our greatest unmet needs. So the greatest mistakes that we make out of our deepest voids are usually made out of our unhealthiest reactions to what is absent and why.

For me it was not the voids that I did not know I had, but rather the voids from where I had lived for years believing that it was my duty in life to manage everyone else's voids. While of course I kept self-medicating out of the pain of wishing that someone else would understand my voids. It was as if my punishment for making certain regrettable mistakes was that I now had to give up my right to be understood or even loved for that matter.

Solving self-medication is about solving pride. The pride that assumes that we could function indefinitely and effectively out of the compounding weight of deeply unmet needs and dry environments void of enough love. While at the same time, assuming that we can somehow manage our most healthy and competent attitudes and behavior.

So, in my own procrastination of pain, I was functioning with a far less honesty about the core of it then the obvious abusive reactions that I was demonstrating as a result of it. Self-medication comes from carrying pain we are not honest about, not pain we are unaware of.

That is why pain can trap us for years. When our insight as to the specific ins and outs of it is a level two, but our conduct as a result of it is a level eight.

So, I stopped. No, not in some warm fuzzy epiphany moment. I was in the same neutralizing orphaning situation all over again, except this time I made the decision to gut it up enough and take a different approach.

Yes, I still fell victim to certain old coping mechanisms more times than I wished. But that is normal especially when the biggest hooks we have to disarm are usually held in the hands of the people we crave to be valued by the most, but in some cases never will be.

Not managing pain is not about your right to feel hurt. It is about your right to love yourself enough to not be exploited. Exploited means when other hurting people can manipulate us or attack us from their pain for the purpose of manipulating our pain to fix the things we did not break. All by using the guilt we actually do carry from where our own negative behavior may have broken some things in other areas. However, the only reason that anyone can exploit your pain is because of what they are really exploiting—*your lack of self-respect.*

A lack of self-respect is simply where you have never given yourself permission to be loved, valued, and forgiven. You have never given yourself permission to say, *"No, thank you"* in the faces of the biggest hooks, and those who carry them.

You have, however, given yourself permission to finish your masters degree, get your MBA from Harvard, own your own business, support a family, buy a house, marry a wealthy person, and climb the social and corporate ladders. But never permission to know you.

Not necessarily know you in the sense of who you are, but in the sense of the personal standard you are unaware you have no business living without.

So, achievements and status actually become the external standard that covers up for your internal lack of one. It is actually a usage of prosperity in order to manage insanity.

This exploitation by others is actually a very easy con job to pull off. Simply because of how badly we will take responsibility for why someone or something else is broken just so we can throw enough generosity at the situation to fix it. This is in order to be positively affirmed by those whose acceptance defines too much of our worth, but whose own pain will never be pleased anyhow.

We are usually taught this as children. Even if we had something to do with why something is broken, we cannot fix the past. Which is why the only kind of people who are going to exploit your lack of self-respect will be those still living there.

What does all of this have to do with personal leadership? Since this book now sounds like we have turned into the *Dr. Phil* show. *(By the way, I believe Dr. Phil is a gift from God.)*

This is the reality. *None of us practice effective leadership in any environment until we agree to practice personal decency with ourselves first.*

So, what did I stop managing?

➤ *I stopped managing people.* People's problems, people's opinions, people's acceptance, people's reactions, and people's rumors. I stopped managing my wife, my peers, my audience, my enemies, et cetera. I stopped managing my past. The parts of my past that were robbed from me by evil people that I kept trying to manufacture artificial replacements to by substituting other people in the same positions to fill the holes of.

No, I did not start playing the theme from *Rocky* on my stereo every day. I just stopped managing my unmet needs. And started doing more to manage the kinds of fulfillment that codependence kept telling me I did not have a right to.

I started loving myself enough to put other people's pain back on them who assumed that all I was really good for was taking responsibility for their pain.

I stopped being a paycheck or a rent check, and I started being Konrad.

"You mean you did all of this in one day?" Actually, I started it in one day, and I've been doing more and more of it every day since.

But I could not start this process without realizing how much I was controlling. In other words, my whole picture of love and safety was contained in the people who I believed would love me and protect me better if they were fixed. So in your mind, you have to enlist the control to manage these people, or situations, which at the end of the day is an unreachable goal fueled by unrealistic hope.

The problem is that trying to fix anyone is like a tire with a small leak that sooner or later you have to keep putting air into. Any safety is never permanent, only temporary. So, you live life trying to hurry up and enjoy isolated moments rather than a whole lifestyle.

This is why we burn out in everything from marriage to prosperous careers. Only to hit the easy out button of *"It must not have been meant to be."* We place ourselves under the weight of managing too many parts of our relationships and scenery of our situations that are not our jobs to manage, instead of just managing us.

Then anger sets in because of what we believe that we now have to fix in order to be seen as a better person than the flawed person we have been judged as. The first thing this performance obligation does is usher in enough anger to usher in enough depression over time to eventually silence faith and then silence vision. Then we lash out in the rage of believing we are stuck when in reality, being stuck is a decision before it is a position. It is the decision to coddle fear, whereas getting unstuck is the decision to expose it.

And since we never want the world around us to know just how burnt out we may be, we just create another type of toxic pressure, which is the pressure of window dressing our burnout. Vices, affairs, materialism, et cetera.

For me personally, my gifts would always work despite my pain. I was the golden boy. I could say things, and still do, that few in my religious profession would dare to say.

I could run to the kinds of fires that most would just hide under the table from.

But while my gifts were on center stage, the personal me was dying. Of course, few knew this either because I could make sure they didn't, or many of them were too selfish or needy to care about anything beyond what my gifts could produce for them. *Most of society is like this. It is too shallow to care who a leader is more than they care about what needs a leader can meet for them* It's kind of like the syndrome in sports that you are only as remembered as your last season.

➢ *I stopped managing other people's problems.*

When we manage other people's problems, we make their problems our own. Then we are forced to control their problems to not be problems for us. That fuels rage.

Then we abort potentially great relationships and opportunities only because the view of them through our anger makes them appear bad, not fixable, threatening, impossible, et cetera.

How did I finally get it? I was right back in the same conflict I had found myself in since childhood. Except now I was a long way from childhood.

That is how a lot of painful patterns work. Our behavior as children is developed to cope with them so that by the time we reach adulthood our behavior is adapted to recycle them.

I was orphaned as a child and still at forty I was being told to manage orphaned situations all over again.

So, what we are built to go through just keeps repeating itself. And in our pain we assume or hope that one day we will be old enough or successful enough that those patterns will have run their course and magically just fall away. Unfortunately, they don't. It is only where we stop managing our involvement with them that becomes the defense to cut them off.

➤ *I stopped managing the low road.* I used to yell a lot. Most people blame that on a personality trait. It's funny because now that I do not yell much at all some of the same people attribute that to me being calmer because I am older. Really I yelled because I felt cornered and powerless; not understood; judged.

Really my powerlessness was based on a level of personal decency I was afraid to enforce, that I was losing more and more of my ability to keep controlling my lack of.

So, I stopped because first of all, it was my responsibility to gain a more truthful perspective of my life then just the lazy perspective that wanted to blame who had not loved me right. Then I began the selfless process of growing bigger than my anger by first giving myself permission to be me.

The ultimate objective of all of this is to change the level of things that can continually derail you. The kinds of situations that you will give your energies to that can cripple you emotionally provoking you to start swinging back with all of the wrong weapons. It is loving yourself enough to change your responses to things.

Our responses to anything say what unhealthy things we will agree to manage and what we won't.

But that is how we get used as the scapegoats for other people's pain. Our negative responses give certain people the unnecessary fuel that allows their issues to stay in hiding and ultimately in control. It's people who do not take responsibility for their own dysfunction who will only use your dysfunction against you.

In other words, our mistakes are their power. So, they never have to deal with who they are as long as your unhealthy reactions maintain the smokescreen they use to hide behind you.

Please know one thing: not managing the wrong things anymore does not mean that the wrong things will still not bother you. You have a right to be bothered by a lot of issues that tear at your heart and your emotions.

But changing what you manage simply means that you change where your energies go. It does not mean that you are now an infallible robot.

By not managing, I was now forcing every hurting relationship and frustrating circumstance to come up to the high road where I now was. This is because of where we manage the wrong things, we can only manage them on the low road. And the only thing we do on the low road is multiply pain, not solve it. *The low road is where we make conflicts into something more than what they have to be so that we can avoid the big picture of what they really are.*

It's like a man I was counseling one day who had shifted the attention off of what were the real problems of his troubled marriage. He did this by trying to accuse his wife of seeing another man.

I told him it didn't matter if she was seeing a hundred other men, the big picture was about what he kept refusing to do to meet his wife halfway and fix their marriage.

The low road is where we take our conflicts personally. So, anything about the person we could be is put on hold while we defend ourselves or lash out in the defiance of the person we are afraid that we are.

Our problems with fear, anger, and trust become the lures that lead us there.

And the secret of conquering the low road trap is to determine what your low road is before you are already on it. In other words, be honest about the destructive games that you know you play on the low road before you are there.

And what is the high road? What it's not is a false humility. The pious, *"I just chose to take the high road."* If you have to always advertise that you took the high road, chances are you are not on it.

The high road is a place where our purpose in life is protected from everything that could only derail our purpose. You cannot fuel conflict and take the high road.

The big hurdle however, will be how you process when other people do not believe about you what you want them to believe about you. Or when circumstances have portrayed you as being more incompetent looking than you believe you really are.

How do we get off of the low road? I can explain it one way like this.

One day in a restaurant with my family, a little girl at the table in front of us became ill and vomited up what she was eating. Her mother rushed her to the bathroom. However, what happened after that was the bigger problem.

I watched waiters and waitresses observe the problem and comment to each other about it. They even pointed it out to other coworkers even in a humorous way. Nobody did anything to attend to the situation. The problem just sat there in plain view of everyone else eating around that table. After approximately five minutes, a busboy came out and cleaned it up.

Society is full of people just like this. They are content to notice problems, comment about problems, and talk to everyone else doing nothing about the problem. Rarely does anyone really speak up.

This is because of what low road people do; *they don't speak up, they just speak sideways.*

Huh? Low road people do not speak up for the solution of anything directly with the source of the problem. They speak to everyone else second and third removed from the problem.

Most people do not even speak up for themselves until they have absorbed so much pain that they erupt. Then nothing is changed because they only exploded about it. So, any decisions that are made are not solutions. They are simply escapes for anger.

Or, just like the wait staff in this restaurant, they are both enchanted with the gory controversy of what it is, that they never think in terms of being a part of the solution for it. Or, they are afraid of what the real solution would require of them to step up in.

When you speak up, you finish the task of something.

When you speak up, you take ownership to make something better than what it is. When you speak up, you also save yourself from storing everything that you will explode about later. You don't have to have an attitude to speak up. People only have attitude when they have insecurity, not clarity.

➢ *I changed my responses to repetitive conflicts.*

We only repeat what we keep handling negatively the same way.

Now I could tell you not to breathe life into the types of situations and behaviors of other people that need to die, and that would be sound advice. But to take things a step further try something that cured me; *don't breathe life into anything that is not the big picture of the circumstance.*

In other words, keep the issue of any situation in front of you and don't allow yourself to go down all of the rabbit trails that at the end of the day cannot resolve the issue. It is only where you will not solve the real issue of any circumstance that you will just be managing the way it has always been. This is one reason why so many people's idea of conflict resolution actually comes out as conflict punishment.

All turnaround in anything begins with today. So, how long something has been messed up and all the reasons why it was, stop at today.

➢ *Do not be impatient when you have to repeatedly guard yourself from the same traps with the same situations or the same people.* I did not master this in one day with one person. My traps kept coming back some days every hour on the hour.

Why? They are determined that if they are persistent enough, they can force the old you back into existence. And if they succeed, then you feel demoralized and quit.

All traps live and die by their ability to use the old you as fuel. Don't let them. It will get easier. Some traps have to turn up the heat before they will disarm themselves by your same healthy responses.

➢ *I stopped managing other people's changes.*

You will never manage your changes and someone else's changes also, so manage your own changes only. Managing yourself only will be the only way that nothing about your circumstances can ever back you into the corner. It's only in the corner that we make our worst decisions.

Part of mastering this will come by managing three things:

1. Managing your own sanity. Let what is insane for other people stay insane for other people. Don't fall into insanity trying to control their insanity.

You will be amazed at how much emotional weight you lose the moment you are no longer managing what is only deception and hurt for other people but isn't deception and hurt for you. So, don't feel like what someone else vomits up from their pain, requires you to vomit up the same thing just to respond to it.

2. Manage the hand you are dealt. Play the card that the situation deals you at the time. Just don't try to overspeculate what you believe the next card will be.

Don't fight with people who have time to play games. People play games because they are not solving the problem.

3. Don't manage the surface. You will never stop managing the wrong things until you can stop managing surface things. Drama lives on the surface.

And any response that keeps you moving forward will be a truth response not a drama response.

➤ *Lastly, I stopped managing who I had no future with and started managing who I did.*

Jesus was a genius at this. *First of all, Jesus determined a relationship by its future more than its commonality.*

For example, Peter, His own disciple hurt Jesus. All betrayal hurts. However, the Pharisees who were of His own culture and who were supposed to recognize Him through the words of their own prophets as their Messiah, hurt Him too.

Both Peter and the Pharisees demonstrated more insecurity than they did leadership most days, but you saw Jesus working with Peter and not with the Pharisees because of one reason: *He had a future with Peter despite His disappointments with Peter. He had no future with the Pharisees.*

Secondly, Jesus did not drag anyone into His future who was not supposed to be there. You can always tell yesterday people by how much it feels like you are dragging them into being today people.

Today people walk. Yesterday people have to be carried. That is usually how we tell the difference between the two. And usually we don't drag people because of the fear of letting go of them. We drag them because of the fear of becoming something better ourselves to attract different people.

Yesterday people versus future people are determined by what we instinctively put into them. Meaning, none of us will ever instinctively put anything good into a yesterday person except when we are trying to control a yesterday person to be a tomorrow person.

Thirdly, Jesus did not rate a relationship by need. He rated them by hunger. There was a woman who had a daughter who was demon possessed. She approached the disciples of Jesus and asked them for Jesus' help with her daughter. They told her to go away, that she was annoying.

She persisted until Jesus finally talked with her, and for the moment made things worse. He told her she was unqualified because of His purpose versus her natural cultural qualifications. When she would not go away, Jesus finally said, *"I cannot throw the children's bread to the dogs."* Instead of this girl storming off in a rage of offences, she paused and said back to Jesus, *"True Lord, but even the dogs get the crumbs off of the master's table"* (See Matthew 15).

Jesus was astounded at her faith and He healed her daughter. The point being that Jesus rejected her for her need, but He responded to her because of her hunger.

You cannot grow with needy people. Everyone has needs. Needs do not qualify a person. You can only grow with hungry people. Hungry people are qualified by action.

Jesus did not even feed the five thousand with two loaves and five fishes because they were in need of food. He fed them because of how far they pursued to listen to Him and the three days they stayed until He was through speaking. *When the foundation of rela-*

tionship is determined by need, codependence will be used to sustain the relationship. And the only thing that fuels codependence is fear. In fear, I have to manipulate you better than you manipulate me.

Fourthly, Jesus chose relationships based on His assignment. I said this in a previous chapter, but it bears repeating. *You don't just connect with a person; you connect with their vision or their lack of one.*

When Jesus chose His disciples, He did not choose them because of everything great that they were. He chose them for two reasons: *His future and theirs.*

Jesus would stop for certain poor and sick people who were begging to be healed, but He wouldn't stop for the elite of His day who were just trying to catch Him in a lie. It wasn't because Jesus had a soft side for the sick or He had some vow of poverty against people who were rich. The sick and afflicted were crying out for something that Jesus could relate to: *His purpose.*

Our assignment has to be bigger than what we can clone from someone else. So the smaller our worldview the smaller the relationships we will choose to fulfill it.

And the moment we choose relationships for what we can clone, we reduce our playing field by more than two thirds.

Lastly, Jesus never measured people by their potential, but by their price to achieve greatness.

One thing that I tell leaders about measuring the difference of those around them between who are worthy of promotion versus those who are not is *never open any doors for anyone who is not trying to kick them down.*

This narrows down the pool pretty quick.

People that only put hundred-dollar effort into a million-dollar dream really only have a hundred-dollar dream. We will never have productive futures with time wasters and with those who are better at talking than doing.

Where is your behavior or personal integrity off course with where you need to be in this area?

____

____

____

____

____

____

____

How would the person you want to be handle this area differently?

____

____

____

____

____

____

____

**Leadership does not manage a plan.
It manages a goal.**

27

KEEPING YOUR HEAD IN THE GAME.

Champions do not just win the games where they had the lead. They win the games where their focus was on something greater than just being behind in the score.

This is because all winning comes down to understanding this fact: *You don't prepare to win. You adjust to win.* So, quitting is simply where you have lost sight of your end result; it is not about where you have messed up.

Which is why preparation only gets you into the game. What you do with what you did not prepare for determines if you win the game.

And do losers prepare less? Not really. Losers often times only lose their drive to overcome what was not in their game plan, which becomes the deciding element that costs them the game.

CEO FACT:

Keeping your head in the game will come down to how much you submit yourself in pressing times to either listening to the coach or the fans.

Fans are different than coaches. Fans want you to win. Coaches provoke you to win.

Fans expect you to be on top. Coaches prepare you to be on top. And while you will need cheer-leaders to support you through tough times you will need coaches to grow you bigger than tough times.

Fans want your autograph. Coaches want your heart.

Fans will boo you when you disappoint them. Coaches will confront you when you disappoint yourself.

So when it comes to understanding the influence between who coaches us and who cheers us in life, the average person does not have enough unbiased counsel in their lives during critical times. They have fans.

Fans, in other words, are other people who possess support value but no challenge value. Mostly because the bulk of their encouragement comes from weaknesses or obstacles they themselves have never stepped up enough to overcome.

CEO FACT:

You will only live with a small vision where you live with a small you.

Ask yourself a question: *how much of your potential success do you spend time talking yourself out of?*

Moses had this problem. God would tell Moses about the leader he was called to be, and Moses would remind God about the leader he couldn't be.

You must remember at all times: *God knew what you were when He called you. And anything that God calls you to finish will always be bigger than what you currently are.*

So, the issue with goals is not about setting them. It is about what you are willing to enlarge about yourself to achieve them. Any great goal is only a great goal when it is currently beyond your control. So, any goal that is only on your current level is not a goal; *it is a safety net.*

This is why many people have never expanded their vision for something greater than what they have; *they have never expanded who they are.*

So, the vision for having better does not work because we imagine it can. It only works when a more functional us lines up with a more expanded vision.

This is because your vision will not get bigger; you will. A bigger you is the only way you can see a bigger picture of what already exists that the narrow parts of you cannot currently see.

CEO FACT:

Where you struggle to put your foot down for what is right will only be because of what you still enjoy participating in that is wrong.

Increase is not what happens when your opposition changes, but rather when your limitations do. So, the struggle to change is not about difficulty, but about resistance—your own. Meaning, people do not struggle with change, they struggle with wanting to. So, you will only plateau anywhere that you will not pay the price to leave.

And all change is the fruit of decision, not difficulty.

The difficulty comes in when we have to pay the price to retrain our character to live without the dependence on anything that was inappropriate or restricting.

And the struggle? It is only the indicator of adapting to what is easiest to control more than it is impossible to overcome.

1.

Tighten up.

Sloppy thinking, sloppy behavior, and sloppy attitude are as bad as a sloppy office, a sloppy car, and a sloppy closet. *You have not prepared to succeed in anything until it is managed in its most organized state.*

Sloppiness drains your environment. It also forces you to battle against disorientation. Which is why people do not bog down in ruts or setbacks. They bog down in sloppy thinking and behavior. Sloppiness just gives credibility to what a rut or a setback is permitted to be. So you will never leave a rut or a setback that you are not willing to jam into the gear of overdrive in your discipline, organization, and perspective in order to propel yourself out of it.

2.

You will have to remove anything about yourself that makes it harder to fight.

Staying in the game is about being married to a goal, not a plan. So, you must protect your movement more than you protect your fear of losing.

Keep exercising. Keep working on a project. Keep playing your favorite hobby or sport. Keep sowing into your family, kids, friends, et cetera. Keep teaching someone. Keep going to your favorite restaurants. If you need to rest or escape, okay. Just don't shut down.

3.

Lower your threshold for pettiness.

Big dogs never chase little bones. Solomon said it this way: "*It's little foxes that spoil the vine*" (See Song of Solomon 2:15). Enough said.

4.

Start being a celebrator of what you complete and not just what you begin or just what you did not mess up.

No matter how successful you are when you die there will always be someone who opposed your success and a personal weakness that worked overtime some days to keep you from it.

It's like this: *Everybody is a friend until you disappoint them and every weakness is an ally until you trust it.* So, being a finisher is not about having always been right or liked. It is about not quitting in the midst of making necessary changes to fix what can be fixed and reconcile what can be reconciled. While at the same time moving on without regret from everything you can't.

Where is your behavior or personal integrity off course with where you need to be in this area?

How would the person you want to be handle this area differently?

In Closing . . .

What is your photograph of a prosperous you?

This question from a therapist friend of mine one day sent me reeling in thought and bewilderment.

I mean it's kind of hard to assume that you and I can achieve a dimension of a fulfilling state in any area that we do not even have a picture of what it looks like.

How would we know we had it or still didn't?

For me personally, I started making a scrapbook of what the next seasons of my life needed to look like.

What the spiritual me, the personal me, the physical me, the friendship me, the married me, the parental me, the leadership me, the financial me, the material me, the hobby me, the vacationing me, and the legacy me needs to look like.

Singles can implement what the dating them looks like in addition to what they want the married them to look like. *Anybody can look at lack, but not everyone can look at prosperity before they achieve it.*

So you will be shocked by what things become familiar in your life when they have become familiar in your sights first.

Secondly, what is the priority? Your priority is usually built around your greatest void.

For me, I had spent much of my life thriving outside of my personal home life, but was orphaned at home.

So, I put my foot down that I was no longer going to be great everywhere else but alone, orphaned, and unstable at home. I was going to have a harbor, an oasis of love, and warmth in my personal life as the foundation first. Then everything else I achieved would spring from that.

This is also how you can identify that you are growing—*by the healthier and more stable things that you see as the solutions to your deepest problems.* Things that center you and stabilize you instead of just medicate you.

Did I immediately achieve that? Nope. But what I enabled myself to do was immediately restructure my values and my priorities which restructured my lifestyle, which sculptured my decisions. All this around establishing the foundation of what would prosper me as a centered person, rather than just as a successful public figure.

Right priorities make right decisions very easy.

BLESS SOMEONE'S LIFE TODAY!!!

Here is your chance to place not one, but two life-changing resource tools into the life of someone else.

For a limited time only, you can purchase not just one additional copy of the book *Turnaround CEO*, but also two (2) additional copies of Dr. J. Konrad Hölé's inspirational devotional, *The LIFECHANGE Promise Book* and at direct from the publisher at a price of only $10.00 for all three books (add $5.00 per packet for shipping and handling).

The LifeChange Promise Book contains 70 topics and over 550 Sriptures taken from the Amplified Bible and is a great gift idea for friends and family, but also an incredible gift source for your local church outreach, event, or organization.

Just fill out the coupon on the next page and mail your order direct to the publisher. Postage and/or shipping will be added extra to the total price. (Please see chart for pricing.)

For faster service you can e-mail your order direct at www.worldcentreministries.org or call: 1-888-522-9699

ORDER FORM

I WOULD LIKE TO ORDER ___ PACKETS THAT INCLUDE BOTH TURNAROUND CEO and THE LIFECHANGE PROMISE BOOK AT ($10) TEN DOLLARS PER PACK.

Name______________________________________

Address____________________________________

City_________________________State______Zip____

Phone_____________________________________

Method of Payment:
(CASH NOT RECOMMENDED)

Check ______ Visa ______ MC ______

CHECKS must be written to *THE WORLDVIEW LEADER* and must include the shipping cost in addition to the total number of books ordered. Please include five dollars per packet for postage.

CREDIT CARD PHONE ORDERS: Call 1-888-522-9699.

☐ Visa ☐ Mastercard

Credit Card #________/________/________/________

Exp._____/______

Total Charge

# of packets ________@	$10.00 each	________
Shipping at $5 per packet	Shipping	________
	Total	________

Signature__________________________________

(See shipping information on next page.)

SEND TO

The WorldView Leader

P.O. Box 41010

Minneapolis, MN 55441